All the Pieces

by Mary E. Twomey

Editorial

Mary Twomey

Steven Lawrence Hill Sr.

ASA Publishing Company

A Publisher Trademark Title page

Published *by*
ASA PUBLISHING COMPANY & Bookstore
P.O.Box 294 Wayne, Michigan 48184
www.asapublishingcompany.com
administration@asapublishingcompany.com
Ph: 734.238.0515 Fax: 734.238.6592

Book: All the Pieces
Date Published: 10.08 / 1st Edition
Book ID: ASAPCID4130976

Physical Warehousing Distribution
ASA Publishing Company

ISBN: 978-0-615-26064-8
Library of Congress Cataloging-in-Publication Data
This book was published in the United States of America.
State of Michigan

A Publisher Trademark Title page

For my husband, Matt
God bless the man stuck with me.
Who could hold a candle to your strength?

For my parents, Bruce and Martha
For buying countless notebooks so I could write stories they were never allowed to read.

For my siblings, Brian, Bruce and Michelle
For pushing me over the edge and encouraging me to work harder.

For the record,
My dad is a great man who, thankfully, was not my inspiration for the father in this book.

ALL THE PIECES

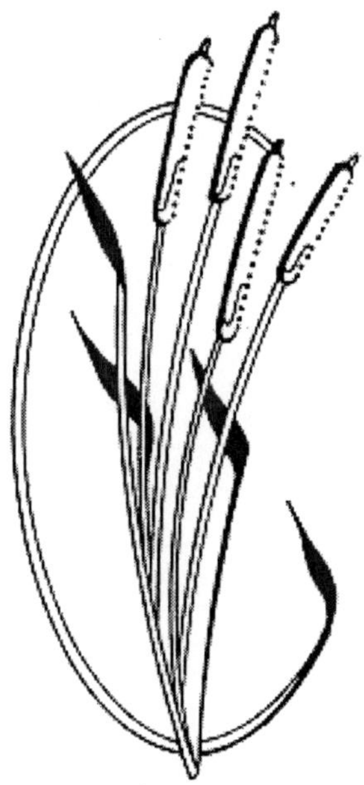

I peaked around the corner and saw
My body standing.

I did not recognize myself.

I did not know who I was.

Chapter One

"Eesa-bel! Where did you put the peanut butter?" RJ yelled from the tiny kitchen. Not only did RJ feel the need to yell everything, but he also felt that 7:30 in the morning was the appropriate time to discuss basic kitchen whereabouts. His sister Isabel rolled over on her soft down comforter, moaning loudly. If it wasn't the peanut butter, then it was the keys, the television remote, the toothpaste, and on more than one occasion, his boxer shorts. Even though Isabel was two years his junior, she still was responsible for the well-being of the apartment, and apparently, her brother and his illusive peanut butter.

"Eesa!" RJ shouted. Usually his shouting closely resembled a dog barking. Isabel regretfully opened her eyes and thought back to the last time her brother had the peanut butter. *Where had he put it?* "It's in the spice cupboard, RJ." She heard cupboard doors opening and closing (remembering that RJ did not cook, let alone use any of the spices), followed by silence.

Blessed silence.

Rolling back onto her side and burrowing herself under her mass of covers, Isabel closed her eyes and prayed for sleep. "Ee-sa-bel! Have you seen my cell phone?" RJ called.

"Men are helpless." Isabel grumbled as she savagely tore the covers off and angrily stomped into the living room. "RJ, did you plug it in last night?" She asked, hands on her hips.

"No. I don't see it." RJ scratched his head in true caveman decorum.

Isabel yawned and pushed her long, thick, black, tangled hair back away from her face. "Did you leave it at Geoff and Jordan's?" She inquired, growing impatient. She tapped her neatly cut fingernails onto her thigh as she leaned against the cold wall.

RJ shrugged as he lifted up a couch cushion, searching for the black cell phone. As he put the green seat cushion back in its proper place, he answered, "I don't know. Maybe."

"Well if you don't know, then how should I? I don't follow you around all day." Isabel glanced once more over the apartment, and then turned back towards her bedroom.

"Come on, Eesa! I have to get to work." RJ called to his sister's back. This morning was not all that different than the morning before, where RJ showcased himself as the patron saint of insensitivity and blame laying. RJ was just in his usual rush, tripping over people and hurrying to get the day started. The tall Italian was something of a workaholic. He worked six days a week as an engineer for General Motors automobile company. His focus on only his work advanced him early on in the company, putting him at the second in command of the engineering department. At twenty-seven, RJ was one of the youngest engineers in his division. Whatever time he did not spend at the office, he spent either working at home or at the gym, boxing out the pent-up aggression that comes from sitting at an office all day.

"I am not your maid. Find it yourself." The sassy little sister slammed her bedroom door shut in hopes of blocking out the rude awakening. She did not start her day until ten o'clock. Today was Friday, and Fridays she spent her day working at the animal hospital, the shift starting at noon. Her bed was her haven, and as she climbed in, she felt the warmth of sleepiness envelope her. As her eyelids began to grow heavy, the front door opened and shut with a bang, as if on cue. Inwardly whimpering, she pulled the stark white covers over her head and prayed for quiet.

"You ready to go, RJ?" Jordan asked Isabel's brother. Jordan worked under RJ at GM. They would meet each other in the morning and drive together to work every day. Jordan lived in the two-bedroom apartment across the hallway from RJ and Isabel's apartment with his best friend, Geoff. Dropping a freshly toasted bagel on the countertop (which also served as the kitchen table, as RJ used the table as his desk), Jordan lowered his voice, "RJ, do you guys have any strawberry jam?"

RJ broke his gaze from searching under the couch to look up at Jordan. He was still fishing for his missing cell phone. "Of course we have strawberry jam. Eesa lives here." RJ stood with no cell phone.

Jordan located a half-empty jar in the refrigerator and spread the jam over the hot, freshly toasted bagel, causing the jam to melt instantly. He pulled a small paper plate down and wiped up the stray crumbs with a napkin from the black napkin holder on the counter. Isabel was Jordan's favorite friend, so it was no surprise that he visited her every morning before work. Leaving the plate on the counter, Jordan walked to Isabel's bedroom, pausing at the door. "Hey RJ," he dug into his jacket pocket and tossed the black cell phone in RJ's direction. "You left it at our place last night."

"Aw, thanks Jordan. Hey, are you ready to go?" He asked, on the move as usual.

"Almost." Jordan smiled as he turned the knob to Isabel's room. Opening her door slowly, he came in and sat quietly on her pillow. "Good morning, Sunshine." Jordan teased, aiming his conversation at the lump under the covers he assumed to be her head.

Isabel burrowed herself deeper under her down comforter and layers of sheets. "Go away. I still have three hours of sleep left." She whined. "Doesn't anyone get that?"

Her friend pulled the mountain of covers back to reveal her messy mass of black hair. Digging his arms under the blankets, he wrapped them around his treasure and pulled her up into his lap. Jordan loved to hold Isabel every morning before work. He would rock her back and forth to relax himself before a long day of work (and dealing with RJ). Cradling her tiny body in his large, safe arms, he smoothed her ragtag hair away from her face, revealing a grouchy expression. "Eesa, if I didn't wake you up, then you wouldn't get to see me before work." He consoled her morning attitude.

Snuggling her nose in his neck, she breathed him in and let herself exhale in his strong arms. As much as she hated waking up three hours too early, she did enjoy seeing Jordan in the morning. Fiddling with his blue and green striped tie, she sighed quietly. "Oh, fine."

"I brought over breakfast for you." He sang, trying to entice her out of bed.

"Did you?" She tried to fight back her smile, but it was no use. She loved him, and was too comfortable in his arms to put up much of a fight.

She usually hated letting go of her ten o'clock morals.

"Just for you, Bel." He smiled back, kissing her forehead with his warm lips.

"Hand check!" A familiar voice teased from the doorway. He was quite a picture, leaning in the doorframe with his arms crossed over his chest. "Good morning, children." His green eyes twinkled.

"Hi Geoff. You off to work too?" Isabel asked. Geoff jogged around to the other side of the bed, hopping onto the other pillow. He took Isabel from Jordan's arms and supported her in his own, squeezing her tight.

"No, I just got off. They asked me to work a double yesterday. One of the nurses called in, so I took her shift." He explained.

"Ooo! The new hot one?" Isabel pinched his stomach and grinned.

"Ouch! Stop it, Eesa. I hate when you do that." Geoff squirmed to make the sensation of her tiny pinch go away. "And yes, it was the new hot one. I didn't do it because she's the new hot one though; I did it because I'm still adjusting to being head nurse on the day shift." Geoff's smile practically jumped off of his face, he was so proud. He had been working at the hospital for four years now, and finally he had gotten the recognition he desired. Unfortunately, the recognition came with extra work hours. "I just came home to shower before I go back."

"You're going back? And why did you work the night shift if you're the day manager?" Isabel adjusted her weight in his arms. Geoff was a smaller build than Jordan, so it took a little effort to get comfortable.

"I did mention that she's the new hot one, right?" He grinned his most seducing grin.

"That's great, Geoff. Three shifts in a row? I can't believe you would rearrange your schedule and work three shifts in a row for a girl who doesn't even have a name." She scolded him. Jordan shook his head at his friend in mock disappointment.

"Yes, she does have a name. I just don't happen to remember it." Geoff raised his nose at her. "And look who's talking. The girl who gives up her Friday nights to work with Isaac – "

"...the pretty boy." Both boys sang in unison.

Isabel playfully punched Geoff in the arm and smacked Jordan in the back of the head. "Shut up, you guys. Isaac is a very good veterinarian. I enjoy watching him work with the animals." Isabel protested, scoffing at the two men laughing. Crossing her arms defiantly, she raised her chin at Geoff. "Yeah, well at least I can remember his name." She crinkled her nose at her friends for emphasis.

Ignoring her, Geoff placed his arms under her legs and behind her back, and with one grand motion, he lifted her up and out of bed. Geoff loved carrying Isabel. There was something about it that made him feel more masculine. Geoff was not as muscular as Jordan or RJ, and Isabel was light and easy to lift, which gave his self-esteem a boost. Also, he liked the way his forearms looked when they were pressed up against her. It was one of the few times that he would allow his mind to drift off into a world where the two of them were slightly more than friends. Either way, he took pride in being able to carry the tiny package with ease, and Isabel certainly saw no point in protesting.

He carried her out to the kitchen and sat her on the stool at the counter. Putting his hand over her mouth to ensure it stayed shut, he held her head against his chest. Taking a few seconds to stroke her billowing mess of hair, he lovingly spoke. "Be nice to me. Some of us don't have to work at noon."

Poking his stomach lightly, Isabel sighed. "Some of us didn't agree to work three shifts in a row. And since when is this noon? It doesn't matter what my schedule is, you guys always wake me up when you have to get up anyway." Realizing that she was now physically out of bed, she saw no point in trying to return to her room. Sleep was definitely out of the question.

Jordan glanced at his black-banded watch as he trotted over to RJ's room, giving the door a tap. "Come on, RJ. Let's go." The living room had been officially turned upside down by RJ's quest for his cell phone, and had been left for Isabel to clean up, as per usual. Emerging from his equally chaotic room, RJ grabbed his thigh-length black leather coat off of the sofa and made his way to the outside world. RJ always walked with his broad shoulders hunched forward, taking each step with determination. Even though Bel was two years his junior, he seemed much older.

RJ grunted as he walked out the door, which was meant to be translated as, "Goodbye. Clean up this apartment." Isabel always pictured him saying, "Unga-Bunga." He was always the master of eloquence, mornings being his best hours of communication.

On his way out, Jordan paused at the counter, sliding the barely warm jellied bagel toward Isabel with a wink. He leaned his long torso over the counter to give her cheek a quick kiss. Isabel gave his tie an affectionate tug. "Goodbye, Jordan. I'll see you when I get home."

"Bye, you two crazy kids. We're finalizing the new steering wheel model." Jordan turned dramatically, leaning himself on the door as he opened it. With a devious look over his shoulder, he smirked and gave his best Casanova eyes. “Don’t wait up.” With that, he was gone.

Isabel ran her finger along the side of her bagel, licking the sweet jelly off in semi-deep contemplation. Geoff stood behind her, trying to twist her hair into what he pictured in his mind to be a braid. “When do you have to go back to the hospital, Geoff?” She asked, lifting her bagel to take a bite.

Geoff’s long fingers wove deftly in and out of her hair, as if they were guided by actual knowledge of braiding. Geoff was the youngest child in his family, with five older sisters to dominate the house. Girly things came natural to him, though he had no real understanding of them. Today, he just liked the smell of Isabel’s hair. Taking a long breath and letting himself become overwhelmed by her expensive florally-sweet shampoo and bamboo coconut leave-in conditioner, Geoff lost himself for the moment and let his sense of smell overtake him. *How do girls smell so amazing?* He thought to himself while he looped his fingers in and out, in and out, in and -

“Geoff? When do you have to go back to the hospital?” Isabel repeated, nibbling her bagel. The red jelly slid slowly over the edge of her bagel, and finally landed itself in a big glop on the small white plate below. “Doesn’t your next shift start, like, now?” She droned, picking up the sticky blob with her two fingers.

Snapping back to the land of platonic friendship, Geoff tried his best to ignore the haunting aroma of his friend’s hair driving deeper and deeper into his already tired senses. Shaking his head in an attempt to bring himself back, he thought through his schedule. “I, um... they’re letting me take a late morning since I just finished a double shift. I don't have to leave for a few hours." He paused to think, "But I'm just going to work the full day. Get some heavy overtime." He decided as he took a break from hairstyling to sit in the stool next to Eesa.

"Open." Bel commanded him, and like a puppy, he obeyed. Sticking the last bite of bagel into Geoff's mouth, Isabel kissed his forehead lovingly. "Okay, *RJ.*" She kidded. "Why don't you see if you can work late tonight too? That'll make it, what? Three and a half? Four shifts in a row? Why don't you just speed up your heart attack? That's a great idea, Geoff. Hey, with all of that overtime you're getting, you might be able to afford heart surgery after all!" Isabel exclaimed, clasping her delicate hands together in mock enthusiasm.

"At least when I go down, I'll be in a hospital." Geoff smiled and grabbed her clasped hands in his. "First of all, I won't work late tonight. I probably won't even stay till the end of my shift, so don't worry." He promised, giving her knuckles a tiny kiss. "Do me a favor?" He asked, gently letting her hands go.

"What's that?" Isabel stood up and took her plate to the dishwasher. She grabbed a rag from the sink to wipe the crumbs off of the counter, always wanting the apartment clean.

Running his hands over his tired face, Geoff made his request. "Two things, actually. Please make me some coffee? And don't ever call me RJ, okay?" Geoff smiled. It was a well-known fact that RJ loved work as much as Geoff loved women. Well that was what Geoff, Jordan and Bel thought. RJ did not really ever attempt to do anything else. Sometimes he would play Playstation with the guys, but if he was not at work or at the gym thinking about work, he was at home working on projects for General Motors. He made more than enough money to live on his own in a nice house, but he chose to live with his sister. Maybe he liked living with her because she cooked and cleaned for him. Maybe he did not have time to go house hunting. Or maybe he knew that the only woman who would live with him and take care of him was his baby sister. Whatever the reason, the only life RJ attempted to have existed in his own apartment between a few friends and his only sister.

As Isabel made coffee, Geoff made himself comfortable on the couch. It was already eight o'clock, which meant that Geoff would have to go back to work soon. Isabel loved her few hours alone in the morning after the boys had gone to their nine-to-five jobs. She thought out her day as she stirred milk and three teaspoons of sugar into Geoff's coffee. First she would go to the gym for a while, and then she would go to the vet's office for work. *And I'll be home by eight for dinner.* She thought to herself as she touched her lips to the black mug, taking a sip of Geoff's coffee.

Walking over to him, she handed him his morning addiction. "Thanks, Eesa." Geoff mumbled. Glancing down at the mug, he noticed that there were lip prints on the rim that he knew were not his. "Sick, Bel! Did you drink some of my coffee?" He whined at the glaring bottom lip mark as though it were the representative of all infectious germs and evil bacteria known to mankind. "You know that if you put a little milk and three teaspoons of sugar in it, it will taste the same every time you make it. Why do you have to taste my coffee? Do you know how fast bacteria can spread? Especially bacteria found in saliva!" Geoff moaned as he tried his best to wipe off the lip print left by Isabel's mouth. He shook his head and kept on muttering to himself all of the different ways that bacteria can lead to infection, and how damaging that can be.

Isabel walked behind the couch and wrapped her arms around his neck from behind. His crusades about cleanliness were lost on her when he would flip out about small things like this. She rested her warm cheek against his, which, she noticed, was beginning to grow a prickly shadow. "I'm sorry, Geoffrey." She purred. "It's just that..." she interrupted her sentence by sticking her tongue to the side of his face, and running it from his chin to his temple in one swift, wet lick. Upon retracting her tongue into her mouth, she ran full speed into the bathroom, which incidentally, was the only room with a lock on the door. Clicking it quickly, she burst into laughter while taking in her friend's fits of repulsion and mortification. She frantically turned on the shower to drown him out.

"This is not over!" She heard him cry over the noisy stream of water. Isabel took a long shower, making sure to let each one of Geoff's medical points on the evils of sharing germs wash off of her and float blissfully down the drain. Bopping her head to an imaginary beat, Isabel joyfully used up the last of the hot water. When he had finally stopped ranting, and the only sound she could hear was the pleasant droning coming from the television in the living room, she exited to her tidy bedroom and got dressed. She packed up a backpack with bottled water, her work uniform, and a book to read in case the day proved uneventful. Resting the pack on the carpeted floor in her room, she decided to rejoin Geoff in the living room. Looking on him from her bedroom doorway, he seemed peaceful, as though he had not moved since she left him.

Noticing him watching her, Geoff patted the empty space on the couch next to him. "Come on, Bel. Watch the Jeffersons with me. I love that JJ." Geoff smiled at the television.

"Put your light saber away, Luke." She remarked, sizing him up. "I come in peace." Isabel smirked as she sat down next to her friend. Instead of sitting on his lap or cuddling up beside him, she opted for about a foot of distance between their bodies, just to make sure that he would not try to retaliate. Geoff was wearing his scrubs with the big bleach stain on the side. Isabel hated those pants. Even though they were obviously clean, she knew that Geoff owned about ten more pairs of perfectly acceptable pants in his apartment. "Geoff, when are you going to throw those out? Seriously, do they still let you wear those pants in front of patients? Because if I saw a nurse coming at me who couldn't even do his laundry properly, I might panic." She tried to tear her eyes away from the bleach and focus them on the good old Jeffersons, but the stain just seemed to get bigger the more she tried to avoid it.

"Oh, quit being a baby. The people at the hospital are too busy to care about spots on the uniforms." He sat a little taller as he brushed a stubborn wrinkle off of his leg. "Besides, if they want me to buy new uniforms every time they get stained, then they'll have to start paying me a lot more." He paused and smiled. "Wait a minute, they are!" Still reveling in his own glory, Geoff happily stretched out his arms over his head. Lowering his right arm and coiling it around her neck, he yanked her down into a forceful headlock. "Never lick my face again." He messed up her wet hair.

"Deal!" Isabel shouted, her head buried in his scrub shirt. Slowly, he let her rise from his grip, not forgetting to flick her forehead on its way up.

Before the banter could progress, the guest buzzer sounded. If it had been any other time of day, at least one of them would have gotten off of the couch to answer the door. Since it was still early, Isabel had a hunch just who it could be.

"It's just RJ. He probably doesn't feel like getting his keys out of his pocket." Isabel groaned as she tried to focus on the television show. She then tried to ignore the next three buzzers that sounded.

"Isabel? Are you there?" A low voice came over the intercom. Isabel winced.

Immediately she connected her feet to the ground and walked to the door. Her pink fuzzy slippers pattered softly across the hardwood kitchen floor as she stalked to the intercom button. Pressing it to speak, she answered slowly, "Yes, I'm here Donny. What do you want?" She queried coldly.

The voice came back just as unwelcome as before. "I want you to let me in. I came by to talk to you."

Geoff walked over to Isabel with his arms crossed over his chest in big-brotherly fashion. He gave her a disappointed look and pressed the buzzer to let him in. "Come on in, Donny." He said, still frowning at Isabel. Turning to fully face her, Geoff gestured his hands out into the air. "What was that all about? Why do you have to be on his case all the time? You guys broke up like, a year ago. You'd think you could give the guy a break."

Right. Like I make any of you hang out with your ex-girlfriends, Isabel thought to herself. "Nothing. Never mind. I don't know." She stammered. "Just make sure he leaves when you do, okay?" Isabel fiddled with the strings on her hooded sweatshirt nervously.

Bang! Donny's loud knock sounded on the door, causing Isabel to jump. She quickly retreated into the bathroom. Closing the door behind her, she breathed a sigh of relief. There were not many people whom she despised, and even fewer that she found insufferable, but Donny was definitely that guy. Even as she heard him conversing with Geoff, she felt the sudden urge to carve out a hole in the wall and jump out several floors onto the street below. Only when Jordan was in the apartment did she feel truly at ease. Donny was Geoff's good friend who dated Isabel for three whole months - her personal record. The relationship ended abruptly when she went to surprise him at work and found him kissing a coworker. To cope with the uncomfortable situation, she would hide. She would hide and carry Mace in her purse. But mostly, she would just hide.

"Ee-sa-bel! I'm getting ready to go now, and Donny's coming with me. Come and say goodbye." Geoff called. Donny was such a sweet guy when they were dating, and usually semi-sensitive. He was such a fun, charming person that the boys insisted he stay a part of their life, much to Isabel's vocalized displeasure.

Swallowing and counting to ten, Isabel turned the bathroom door handle and stepped out into the apartment. Geoff and Donny were chatting in the kitchen while Geoff finished his coffee and put on his navy blue coat. "Bye guys. Have a good day at work, Geoff." She tossed half-heartedly as she gathered the dirty dishes into the sink. She avoided eye contact with Donny at all costs. Geoff sighed and walked over to what he thought was a pouting Eesa, but what was really an uncomfortable Bel.

"Come on, Eesa. I'm sorry I snapped at you. Lighten up." He spoke softly as he placed his empty mug into the sink.

Out of habit, she picked up the blue dishrag hanging over the faucet and began to wipe down the already clean counter. "It's fine. Have a good day at work, okay?" She wiped absentmindedly, now avoiding eye contact with Geoff.

Placing his hand on the rag to stop the circular motion, Geoff persisted. "Please, Ees. Come on. I'm leaving and I don't want you to be mad at me." His big green eyes looked down at her, almost pleading.

She turned around to face him, realizing that this was all too dramatic. "I'm not mad at you, Geoff. I guess I'm just tired." Even though it was a half-truth, it seemed to work. Geoff smiled and wrapped his arms around her tiny waist, clasping them around the bottom of her spine. He did this thing only when he would hug her, where he would rub his thumb up and down a few inches where his hands were clasped. Isabel did not know why she loved it so much, but she did. Letting the gentle circular movement of his thumb console her, she sighed deeply. "I'll see you tonight when I get home."

"Okay, sweetie. Have a good day. Don't spend too much time drooling over Isaac, okay?" He teased with a final squeeze, removing his hands from her waist to pick up his backpack from the floor. Slinging the green pack over his semi-sturdy shoulder, he opened the door and lightly smacked Donny on the back. "C'mon, man. Are you going to work this morning?" Geoff corralled Donny to the door.

"Yeah. I guess I should get going. I don't want to be late for my lunch with Max." He spoke just loud enough to leave the hint in Isabel's direction.

Max was the owner of the veterinary office where Isabel worked. When she was still dating Donny, he would come and visit her at work and chat with Max on occasion. Even a whole year after they had broken up, he still felt the need to wedge himself into her life.

When Isabel did not respond to the bait that he left on the table for her to grapple with, he continued to attempt to get under her skin. "Actually I'm heading that way right now. Why don't I walk you there?" He suggested. "He wanted to talk with someone about hiring on some new assistants to prepare for the expansion."

"The expansion isn't until April. How do you figure he wants your opinion about anything? You can't even remember to pay your bills on time. I don't think you know anything about expanding a business, see, because you would have to know how to budget the eight dollars an hour you make at Starbucks." She tried to keep her anger at bay.

"I don't know. I guess he just likes me." Donny shrugged his shoulders as though he had no intention of wounding Isabel with this information. "Let's go." He cocked his head to the hallway.

"Great." Geoff, who had been momentarily forgotten, knocked his fist on the already opened door. "I have to go, guys. See you." He waved as he left, shutting the door behind him.

Suddenly very aware that she was in the apartment alone with her archenemy, Isabel quickly took a step back.

Not noticing her displeasure, Donny continued. "There's going to be a lot of changes going on." He rattled off. "That's what we're discussing today."

"That's great." Isabel heard herself say. "I've actually got to get going soon, speaking of Max." She flushed, turning to go get her black backpack from her room. She took her time zipping up the bag, as she hoped he would go away by the time she returned to the living room.

"I know you don't have to work for a while, but I'll wait for you anyway." Donny called as he walked into living room, making himself at home.

Coming out into the living room, she dropped her bag with a thud onto the floor. The air was always uncomfortable to Isabel when Donny was around. The charm she used to find adorable now felt suffocating, and left a terrible taste in her mouth. "That's okay. I'm actually leaving now to go to the gym. I don't know that you'd feel like waiting for an hour and a half."

Donny kept his gaze steadily on her. "No, I don't mind."

"Whatever. I'm going." Isabel tossed her long black hair and reached for her bag.

"Let me get that." Donny offered, picking it up off the floor. "Let's go." He put his hand on her back to move her towards the door.

Isabel's back burned where he touched her, and she quickly shirked away. "Sorry." She explained. "I just don't like being touched." *By you*, she whispered in her head. When they were dating, he treated her like a little girl. He never let her do things by herself. Though most girls might enjoy having their bags carried for them, Donny used to treat her as though she were incapable of doing anything without his help. Since they had broken up, Isabel relished carrying her bag seven blocks on her own small shoulder. Remembering her independence from him, she took the bag off of his shoulder and slung it over her own. "I can get that." She offered him her short explanation with no appreciation.

Donny's face hinted at sadness. "Fine."

Isabel smiled inwardly. She had just narrowly escaped a long, drawn out screaming match with him. When they were together, they could not calmly disagree, they had to fight and yell at each other. It always struck Isabel as ridiculous when Donny would ask her what went wrong in their relationship.

Isabel kept her back to him as they walked out of the apartment and down the stairs. As far as she was concerned, Donny was always standing too close to her. With every step he took, she felt as though she had to run to get away. "Isabel, slow down." Donny requested, trying to keep by her side. "What's the rush?" He asked as they walked out of the building.

"Nothing, I just want to go. That's all." She felt safer now that they were on the sidewalk surrounded by people. The office was only a twenty-minute walk to the left, and she enjoyed walking each of the minutes alone every morning. Two blocks down the street was her favorite coffee shop (definitely not a Starbucks) where she would stop in and buy a caramel mochaccino with a packet of sugar and a bagel every morning. She almost always paid with a five-dollar bill, and today would be no exception. "Do you think you could wait outside? I just want to stop in real quick." Isabel practically slammed the door shut behind her to finally separate them. Upon being without him, she sighed happily.

The sigh came too soon, she realized, as the door opened behind her. In came Donny, being just as intrusive as ever. "No, I don't want to wait outside." Donny gave her a look that showed what he thought of her. "Go get your coffee." Since it was clear that he would not leave her alone, she decided not to make a scene.

As they walked into the partially busy coffee house, she looked around at all of the customers. By the front window in his usual spot sat Lou, who was a writer. He had a novel published three years ago that never really went anywhere, but that did not stop him from starting another one. For about a year now, Lou would sit alone at the table for two with his thin black laptop computer, and watch the people on the streets walk by him, leaving behind them little pieces of inspiration without even knowing it. Sometimes she would see Lou writing, but most of the time he was just observing.

Then there was Travis who played chess by the rustic fireplace. While Lou was well into his forties, Travis was about Isabel's age. He loved playing chess, and was almost always asking a stranger to play with him. Sometimes she would see him playing a new contestant and she would stop to watch. He never lost a game. Sometimes Isabel would come in and he would be reading a book in his usual comfy chair by the gas-powered fireplace, waiting for someone to play. He liked to read philosophy, and today he was engrossed in a well-worn book by St. Augustine.

As Isabel and Donny walked up to the register, Isabel smiled at Lou, and then ruffled Travis' perpetually scruffy hair. Travis smiled up at Eesa, and lit up when he saw that she had a companion. "Hey Isabel. Who is this?" He asked, temporarily closing his book.

"Nobody." Isabel caught herself. "I mean, this is just a friend of a friend, Donny. Donny, this is Travis." She half-heartedly introduced them. She realized that she had just let Donny into her little coffee shop world, and that she desperately did not want him there.

The two men shook hands as Travis' green eyes sparkled with conversation. "It's nice to meet you, Donny. Do you play chess?" He asked with all of his unabashed geeky revelry shining through.

Donny shrugged his shoulders. "I haven't played chess in years." He spoke, putting his hands in his pockets.

Isabel perked up. "Oh, Travis is great. Why don't you let him teach you?" She suggested, moving him to the chair opposite Travis. "You've got time before your meeting, right?" Isabel pawned Donny off on Travis for a few hours of sanity. The break from her old, poorly lit flame was much appreciated.

After Donny gave Isabel her backpack, he reluctantly sat down to play chess with Travis. Isabel ordered her usual from the menu, got her change back, and with a wink at Riley, the cute college girl who worked the counter, she was back on the street. As she turned to her left, she lightly tapped the glass pane window in front of Lou to wave at him. She sipped her hot beverage as she walked exactly one more block. Here sat Homeless Joe. Isabel did not know his name because his English was unintelligible. Not that he spoke a different native language, but he was so slurred and broken down that Isabel could not understand him. So there he sat, "Homeless Joe" as Isabel had so lovingly nicknamed him, in front of the shoe store by the lamppost. With his cane across his lap and a doll's ripped off head in his right hand, Homeless Joe sat humming a song that only he knew.

Parking her bag on the ground next to him, she tapped him on the shoulder. No matter how many times Isabel talked with him, Homeless Joe always seemed shocked to see her. "Here you go, Joe." She rhymed as she did every morning.

Joe cautiously took the plain bagel from Isabel and bit into it, still staring at her. Isabel loved chatting with Joe. He was like her very own free therapist. He would just eat and listen as she rattled off what was on her mind. Donny, work, RJ... whatever she felt like talking about. Homeless Joe heard and understood every word that Isabel spoke, but had a hard time talking back on account of his malfunctions, and well, the fact that he had about ten teeth left. Homeless Joe had suffered a stroke years ago that made it quite difficult for him to use the left side of his body. That was why he did not bother to speak. He could just barely move the left side of his mouth. However, he could move it just enough to nibble on the bagel that Isabel brought him every morning. He knew that Isabel was special, so to himself (where most of his thoughts stayed) he referred to her as his angel. After all, she did refer to him as "Homeless Joe", so he did not think she would be too adverse to a name change as well. He had grown to like his nickname, and spending five minutes every morning with Isabel was the most conversation he would get all day. He looked forward to her visits, and the bagel she bought for him was sometimes his only meal of the day.

As Isabel told him all about Donny's antics, Homeless Joe took little bites of his bagel and handed Isabel the doll's head to hold. He had found the head while digging through the trash one day, and had decided to keep it. The doll had red curly hair, and it reminded him of his daughter's hair when she was young. He would sit by the lamppost and sing to the doll head and stroke its hair. He missed his daughter, and the doll made him not feel quite so lonely.

"I'm so glad that at least you understand me, Homeless Joe." Isabel had finished venting.

Homeless Joe (whose actual name was Henry) smiled his less than toothy smile as Isabel grabbed her bag and said goodbye to her friend. He nodded and partially waved as Isabel walked away to go to work.

Her stroll to work was beautiful. The leaves were just starting to turn multiple shades of lush fall colors, making everything seem more magical in her mind. One giant, deep breath cleared away all of the mess that she had just vented to Homeless Joe. When she was sure that no one was looking, she did a little hop in the air to celebrate how free she felt.

Since it was only a quarter after nine, Isabel strolled down a block and a half to the gym. On mornings when her plans to sleep in were interrupted, she relished spending her extra time exercising. As she entered the eighteen and older gym, she was greeted by the brunette at the front desk. "Hey Becky, is it crowded?" Isabel inquired as the peppy girl ran her fitness card through the check-in machine.

"Not really. Oh, Lucas doesn't get in until ten o'clock, so you've got time to warm up. Do you want me to put you on his list today? He's clear until eleven." Becky checked Lucas' clipboard. Lucas was RJ's personal trainer, and he also helped Isabel on occasion as well. Lucas really liked to hang around with RJ at the gym because RJ was so quiet and rarely asked for help. The older brother asked him to keep an eye on Isabel at the gym to make sure she was safe and taken care of.

"Thanks, Beck. That would be great. I'll be in the weight room." Isabel put her card away and went to the locker room to store her backpack. She loved coming to the gym while the rest of the adult world was at work. The quiet atmosphere made her workout much more relaxed and productive.

Isabel ran around the track eighteen times before going down to the weight room. She enjoyed running, especially when she was the only one on the track.

There were a few other people in the weight room, but plenty of equipment to go around. Isabel picked a spot in the corner to lift her ten-pound dumbbells. You could tell who the single guys were because they always used the benches near the front, so that they would be visible to the people walking by. The weight room had transparent walls on three sides, with a back wall comprised of cement, then padded with an orangey-reddish sort of color. Isabel sat in a corner with the padded wall, so as not to be disturbed by the jocks. You could tell the difference between the guys who were there for physical fitness purposes, and those who were there to secure their Friday nights. The guys who were just there to work out would keep their eyes to themselves. A meat market man rarely concentrated on his workout, just on the eye candy passing by.

After free weights, she switched to the bench press. As she was benching a third of her body weight and lost in her own thoughts, a loud bass voice interrupted her. "You know you shouldn't do this without a spot, Isabel. Didn't Becky tell you I was coming?" Lucas stood over her and put the barbell back on the hook. The thing about Lucas was that he had no idea how loud his voice actually was. What seemed normal to him made all of the other weightlifters turn their heads to look.

Isabel sat up and stretched out her tensed muscles. "Hi, Lucas." She took a sip of her bottled water.

"Your brother would kill me if he knew that you weren't using a spot." Lucas shook his head at her as if to scold her behavior.

Putting her water back on the floor, Isabel groaned. "It's still morning, and I've already had a long day. I kind of just wanted to be alone today, Lucas. Besides, you let the other members go without a spot if they want to. Just because RJ is my brother doesn't mean that –"

"It means that I want you to wait so I can spot you." Lucas cut her off, holding his hand out to help her up. "Why don't you go down to the pit? You can be alone there. Did you bring your gloves?" The more arguing that snuck its way into the conversation, the louder his voice grew. Isabel thought the pit to be a good option, as it was much better than being the focus of the entire weight room.

Isabel picked up her black neoprene boxing gloves to display them to Lucas. "Ta-da!" She grinned, taking his hand to stand up. She spent the rest of her time at the gym in the boxing area, which was affectionately referred to as "the pit". After punching and kicking for about an hour, it was time for her to shower, and then off to work. The gym was starting to fill up with the out-of-work-I-just-woke-up crowd, so she made as quick an exit as possible.

Upon stepping out of the building, Isabel was greeted by a gust of fresh mid-morning air. It filled her lungs and blew at the little black curls that wouldn't fit into her tightly wound bun atop her head. The veterinarian's office was only six blocks west, so she arrived to work just in time to be fifteen minutes early.

The waiting room was small and cozy. They kept a very sanitary workplace, so the waiting room rarely smelled too terribly of animals. This particular morning there were five appointments to get paperwork ready for, so that was what Isabel set off to do. After donning her white smock, she turned on her computer and pulled out the paperwork she needed for the day. Her filing system worked best when she had no one distracting her. Only Max and one of the doctors named Eugene McPrice were in the back room. Other than those two voices, the office was empty. Isabel loved those first few minutes in the morning where everything was quiet. She worked at organizing the patients' paperwork, which took awhile. The first appointment was scheduled for noon. It was Ms. Donna Sommers and her cat, Mr. Chesterfield. This was Mr. Chesterfield's third visit in two weeks. He was their best customer. Ms. Sommers was particularly protective of her feline, always thinking that something was wrong when there was rarely anything to report. Isabel smiled as she got everything ready for the appointment, including warning Mr. McPrice that Mr. Chesterfield was on his way. Mr. McPrice was a dutifully patient doctor, perfect for any qualms Ms. Sommers would have.

At noon exactly, the little bell above the door rang, announcing the arrival of Ms. Sommers. As the veterinarian's office was as good an excuse as any to dress up, Ms. Sommers came in decked out in a long, flowery Sunday dress with a larger than life yellow hat on top of her head.

Isabel stopped herself from staring. "Good morning, Ms. Sommers. Dr. McPrice will be with you in a minute." Isabel smiled her most polite smile. Dr. McPrice took significantly more than a minute. He was busy preparing himself for the third degree from Ms. Sommers. She had a habit of not believing him when he would tell her that her cat was perfectly healthy. When he finally called her in, he shot Isabel a look and tried not to sigh. She smiled back, glad that she was the veterinarian's assistant, and not the veterinarian.

Getting on with her work, she was so engrossed in organizing the next few patients that she jumped when the tiny bell above the door sounded. The jump turned into a chill as Donny entered the empty waiting room. "Thanks for ditching me." He grumbled, obviously abandoning his ever-popular "making nice" routine. "I almost didn't make it here, that kid is obsessed with playing chess."

"Shame." Isabel kept her eyes on her computer, which was not doing what she wanted. "Max is in back. He's probably in his office." She gave him as little attention as possible.

"It wouldn't kill you to be nice, Bel. I'm trying here." He reverted back to his lost puppy act, complete with slouched shoulders and a "woe is me" sigh.

"But why are you trying? I'm not your girlfriend, and we're not even friends. Could you just have the decency to at least leave me alone after you cheat on me?" Isabel threw at him angrily.

"You know that I promised Geoff and your brother I'd look after you if they let me date you. I'm not about to stop just because you broke up with me." Donny trumpeted the same reason he always gave when Isabel would muster up the courage to confront him. Silence hung in the air as Donny gave her a dejected smile that demanded pity.

Predictable as they come, Isabel bought into the sad eyes and drooping mouth line. Deciding that pawning him off on her friend was not exactly the nicest thing to do, she reluctantly picked up the phone and paged Max to the waiting room.

She tried to ignore Donny, keeping her eyes so focused on her computer that eventually they began to water. A wish for him to leave almost surfaced itself in a silent prayer as she drummed her nails on the keyboard. He had already taken up too much of her day.

Not a moment too soon, Max meandered out into the crème colored waiting room. "Hello, Don. Come on back. I was just thinking about you." Max smiled and shook his hand, bearing the look of "oh, son I never had" to Donny. Isabel tried to ignore them and appeared pleasantly distracted by her computer. They retreated back to Max's office and left Isabel to calm down.

Calm down she did (though it took most of the afternoon), and by the time the last patient checked out, she was singing "Ain't Too Proud to Beg" in her head. Even though Isaac had to work at their sister office that day, it did not stop Isabel from daydreaming about her coworker as she packed her nearly empty water bottle into her backpack.

Punching out was one of the best parts of the day, as far as Isabel was concerned. Although she enjoyed her job at the veterinarian's office, she knew that Jordan was at home making dinner. Her stomach rumbled just thinking about it. The plastic timecard clicked in the machine, and as she picked up her coat and backpack, her boss's voice sounded from around the corner. "Isabel?" Max's distinctive business tone was loud and clear.

"Hi, Max." She answered as she buttoned up her wool coat. As soon as the material grazed her bare neck, an urge came over her fingertips to itch the spot where the neckline was touching her. Trying to ignore it, she fully focused on what Max wanted.

Max stroked his red beard methodically, as though he were still waiting for his words to come to him. "Isabel... Could you come in on... Monday...

'round noon? We are having a meeting about Pet Vet's... future." He trailed off, still rubbing the hair on his chin.

Isabel had to all but staple her arms to her sides to keep from scratching her neck. "Sure." She nodded politely. No sooner had he turned his back, when she violently scratched the back of her neck, glad to be relieved of the dreaded itch.

The sky was darkening when she emerged from the veterinarian's office. Her walk home was more of a trot home, as the season was beginning to change from early fall to late fall. She observed that it was much colder than it had been even a week ago. Though she could not see her breath in front of her, she was still convinced that it would be a bitter winter.

Skipping up the poorly carpeted stairs to her apartment, Isabel unlocked the door and popped in. While she had been expecting all three boys to be laughing and playing Playstation, the apartment was silent. All three men sat somberly in the living room, staring at the floor. They seemed out of place to her, sitting gloomily on the cheery white and pale green couch.

"Hi guys. What's going on? It's so quiet in here." She commented, walking past them to toss her bag into her room. As she went back out into the living room, the air felt strange and almost morbid. "Did you guys eat without me?"

RJ kept his head down, not caring to acknowledge his sister's question. "Sit down, Eesa!" He finally barked. RJ didn't often speak to her so severely, so she knew not to hesitate or argue with him. She sat down quickly on the couch next to Jordan, who noticeably did not pull her closer to his side.

"RJ, what -" Isabel started.

"Just be quiet. I have to talk to you. Sit down." RJ ordered, still not looking at her. RJ was usually a fairly intense individual, but this was too much, even for him.

"I am sitting, RJ." Isabel spoke quietly.

From the pit of his stomach RJ yelled, "I said be quiet, Eesa!" Complete with a pound of his fist on the coffee table, RJ was officially upset.

Slowly, she glanced at the boys. None of them would look at her, and even Jordan who was usually her ally could not look above her anxiously folded hands. Growing nervous at the prolonged silence, she ventured a conversation amongst the wolves. "Okay, tell me what's going on now, or I'm going to my room. This is ridiculous." She shook her head. "Man, nothing is this big of a deal." Even as she said it, she only partially believed that they were over-reacting. While Geoff was known to exaggerate, Jordan and especially RJ were not ones who tolerated drama.

RJ wiped his hands across his face, giving a loud sigh. There was only a digital clock in the living room, but if there had been a regular clock, you would have heard the tick-tocks clear as a bell. The tension was almost too thick to catch a full gulp of air. "Isabel..." RJ's tone was a bit more sympathetic this time. "I've got something to tell you."

Chapter Two

RJ had gone to work that morning same as he had every morning. With Jordan by his side all day long, the workload had been identical to that of all the previous days. RJ liked predictability, and he ran his life by the shiny silver watch on his wrist.

The two boys arrived to work exactly at 8:40 a.m., as they always did. RJ would not tolerate being late to work. He was a bit obsessive, and his punctuality was only the start of it.

There were no pictures in RJ's office. There was no Nerf hoop or golf game set up as all of the other offices had. RJ liked simplicity. The clear space gave him room to think and to do his work effectively. His neurotic system proved worthwhile, as RJ was one of the top engineers in his section. Limited only by his youth, RJ let few other things stop him.

His project for the day was done at noon, so of course he started on the next day's agenda. RJ had to stay constantly busy, though he never seemed flustered by his mountain of work or out of sorts. The steady stream of work was therapeutic for him. The work kept him from thinking about things his mind would not tolerate. It was when he accomplished a project that he truly felt like a man.

At one o'clock exactly, Jordan knocked on his office door, opening it slightly. "Hey workaholic, you ready to take a break? Let's go to Barney's today. He still owes me twenty bucks from last week's poker game." Jordan came all the way in and half-shut the door. Although Jordan enjoyed his job and worked very hard on all assignments given to him, no one's dedication compared to RJ's.

"Sure. Give me a minute." RJ said as he almost always did. Tearing himself away from his work was a process, so Jordan sat down. He relaxed his back in the conference chair, taking the time to twirl and swivel the chair around a few times for entertainment.

On his third twirl, the phone rang. The black phones at work all had the same ring. They all sort of hummed softly as opposed to beeping loudly. "Jordan, could you get that?" RJ asked beneath his stack of memos.

Rolling his eyes, Jordan did a half swivel and turned to answer the phone. "RJ's office; this is Jordan."

The voice on the other end came over loud and clear. "Jordan! How's my baby?" The robust voice brought a smile to his face.

"Hi, Grandma. How are you? We sure miss you." Jordan leaned back in his chair and rubbed his stomach methodically.

You could hear the love in her voice. "Oh, I miss you too, my baby boy. Now where is my grandson?" She inquired.

Of all grandparents in the Northern Hemisphere, she was the best one. She was so small, but her loud Italian voice compensated for her limited stature. Although she was really only RJ and Isabel's grandmother, she had always referred to Jordan and Geoff as her grandsons as well. Jordan had grown up with just his mother, so being adopted into a large Italian family was just what he needed. With a visible smile reflecting in his voice, Jordan answered, "RJ is right here, Grandma. Love you." He handed the phone to RJ, who was beginning to put away his folders.

Taking the phone and tucking it under his chin, RJ continued sorting. "RJ, I need you to sit down." Grandma dictated in her soft tone.

RJ put his folders down immediately and held the phone tight. "I am sitting down. What's wrong?" Every movement stopped, and RJ sat motionless in his chair. If there was one person you did not ignore, it was Grandma. She always meant business when she was serious, and no one hesitated in obeying her.

"Now the hospital has been trying to contact your house, and Father Joseph has been calling the house too. Luckily I am the only one with your work phone number, so I get to tell you the bad news."

"Grandma, you're stalling. What's wrong? Is Grandpa okay? Where are you?" RJ got right down to business.

Grandma laughed her beautiful, hearty laugh. "No, no. Aren't you my sweet boy? Your Grandfather is right next to me. We are both fine."

RJ relaxed his death grip on the phone a bit. "Well, then what's wrong?" By now Jordan was standing and staring at RJ with a worried expression on his face. He leaned in closer to try to eavesdrop on the conversation.

"It is your father, RJ. He passed away this morning." She spoke the strange words.

An entire minute of silence passed before any more words were uttered. When RJ finally opened his mouth, only unintelligible syllables came out. He took a moment to regain his composure.

"Your Grandfather and I will take care of everything, we just need to know if you want a funeral."

RJ's throat had all of a sudden gone dry. "No." He answered. "That, um, that would not be the best idea."

"Your Grandfather said to maybe just have a viewing for his family, if they would want to see him. No one would make a speech or say anything. What do you think of that?"

RJ nodded a few seconds before his mouth actually opened. "That's fine."

"We would love for you to come, RJ, but we will understand if you do not want to go." The grandmother shook her head sadly. "We will understand whatever Isabella decides to do too." She paused before asking the question that she had been dreading since she had picked up the phone to call RJ. "If you want me to tell Isabella, I will." She spoke quietly.

"No. I'll tell her." He said calmly. He began to realize that he had no idea how he would break this to his sister, thus adding another issue to deal with. Softening a bit, he asked, "How... how did he die?" The last word made his throat go hoarse. Even speaking the word chilled him to the core. Floods of conflicting emotions spread throughout him, but there were none that he could actually invest in enough to let himself really feel.

"He had a heart attack in his sleep last night and died in his bed." She paused. "The doctors said he probably was not in much pain." She stopped herself. "Oh, RJ, I am so sorry." A gigantic tear slid down her cheek. "I know he was... but he was not always that way. You poor children! Your poor mother, rest her soul. I am so sorry!" Her solitary tear was joined by several more cascading down her wrinkled cheeks. Her sniffles turned into sobs, and her sobs turned into high-pitched "yilps".

RJ looked as helpless as he felt. Grandparents were the family's most prized possession, so RJ's first concern was not how he would deal with his father's death, but how his grandmother was handling her son-in-law's death. His next concern still was not himself, but how his sister would react.

Grandfather took the phone from his wife, and RJ could tell that he was holding her. "RJ? This is your Grandfather." He spoke over his wife's yilps.

"Hello, Grandpa. Don't worry. I'll take care of Isabel. Tell Grandma that I will see her at the viewing. Do you know where it will be at?" RJ hurried the particulars so that Grandpa could attend to his beloved.

"It is at St. Paul's funeral home on Monday. That is down the street from your old Catholic church." Grandpa continued to caress the stringy tendrils of his wife's grayed hair. "Yes, RJ. You are a good son. We hope to see you there." He lowered his voice slightly, rocking his tiny wife. "Goodbye, grandson." He hung up the phone.

Suddenly carrying the weight of the entire world, the exhausted man sat back in his chair, his eyes wide open. Moments upon moments flashed through his mind, making his head spin. There were no words.

"RJ... what happened?" Jordan stepped forward cautiously. "Is Grandpa okay?" The worried expression on Jordan's face did not even compare to the turmoil going on in RJ's stomach. Sores that had been healed for years began to aggravate once again along his stomach lining. The transition was almost instantaneous.

Clenching and unclenching his fist a few times, RJ finally answered, keeping his voice painfully low. "It's my dad." He swallowed down the lump in his throat. "My dad died." Even as he said it, that strange word echoed in his head.

Dead.

Jordan's mouth went dry. *Dead.* "Are you going to tell Isabel?" He jumped to his immediate concern.

RJ nodded slowly, and didn't stop nodding for a full minute and a half. *Dead.* "I don't even know where he's been living since he got out of jail. I don't... know..." RJ trailed off, staring into the oblivion ahead of him. Of all the things to think about, of all the things to tell her, death was the one thing they were not prepared for. Out of state? Sure. But dead? *Dead.* He went back to oblivion.

"Do you want me to go get her? I'll talk to Rick." Jordan insisted, moving to the door. As his hand touched the knob, RJ snapped back into life.

"No!" He raised his voice, standing up halfway. Jordan stopped and turned to face him. Quieting his tone a bit, he restated his command. "No, Jordan. Let her finish out the day. It'll be the last normal one she'll have for a while." He stopped to think, and then decided to sit back down. "She works late tonight, doesn't she?"

Jordan thought for a moment. "Yeah, it's Friday. We'll beat her home by a few hours." Isabel got home late on Friday nights, so Jordan (and usually Geoff) sacrificed Friday nights to make dinner for her and hang out.

"Okay. Then I'll just tell her when she gets off of work." RJ paused to run his rough hands over his desk. "No big deal." He told himself, finally resting his palms flat on the top of the shiny mahogany desktop.

Jordan ruffled through some loose papers on RJ's desk. "I can finish up any work you have left for today." He hinted. Not the best at taking hints, RJ gave him a puzzled look. Jordan put his hand flat down in the middle of the desk. "Go home, RJ." He stated with subtle authority.

Not at all accustomed to taking advice or hearkening to authority, RJ's puzzled expression turned into a rushed scowl. "I have work to do. I can't go home." He pulled out the documents he had just put away and spread them all over his desk in a slapdash manner.

"No, RJ. Go home. Take a nap. Call your family. I'll even call Rick and tell him I am going with you." Jordan insisted. Getting on his knees and begging would not have done any good. RJ was a determined machine.

"Jordan," RJ paused his mad dash to work and began massaging his temples, "I'm not you or Geoff. Isabel and I don't like to think about this kind of stuff. If I am working, I don't have to think about any of this. Just let me deal with this the way that I want to." RJ picked up his pencil and began to review his prints with a shaky hand. Jordan did not move. The tension in the room built until you could actually feel the second hand on the clock ticking, pounding with every stroke. "Jordan, just go to lunch without me. I'll be finished by five. I just really want to get these prints approved by the end of the day." RJ could not bring himself to look at his friend.

Being that he worked with RJ, Jordan knew that there was no project that could not wait until the next week to be approved. Nodding, as if accepting the lie, Jordan shrugged his previously tensed shoulders. "Okay, RJ. I'll see you at five." Not quite sure as to what he should do, Jordan turned around and exited to his own workspace, not really caring for lunch anymore.

The day passed slowly for Jordan, checking his watch every five minutes as he waited to go home. Patience was never his strong suit. The rest of his day was spent thinking of ways to cushion the blow for Isabel. He was obsessing, actually.

The rest of RJ's nine-to-five was spent working his heart out. His black wall clock read 4:55 by the time he had finished the entire load of Monday's work, causing a tremendous amount of strain to his stomach. This pleased the workaholic because the viewing was on Monday, so he would not be behind at all.

Just before the time turned to five o'clock, RJ picked up the phone to make the dreaded call to his boss to request Monday off of work. RJ never requested days off. Even as his finger dialed Rick's extension, RJ was still mentally debating if he really needed to take the entire day off.

"Stetson." The loud voice came over the phone, interrupting his train of thought.

"Yeah Rick, it's RJ." He took a long breath before making his speedy request. "I'm going to need Monday off of work." He spat it out as though the sentence were one word, exhaling from the stress building up.

From the other end of the phone, Rick postured. He answered immediately. "Done. Go." Rick was a busy, but fair boss, and he noticed RJ's hard work. It was common knowledge around the office that nothing could pry RJ away from his desk, short of a natural disaster.

RJ was surprised at how quickly his boss had consented. With the phone in his left hand, he rubbed his tensed shoulder with his right hand. "At least let me put up a fight, Rick. Don't make this too easy on me. I may just decide to never come back, and then what would you do?" He joked. Joking did not come naturally to RJ, but his normal personality had taken the backseat.

"So what happened? House burn down? Dog die?" Rick laughed, enjoying this new, lighthearted RJ.

RJ exhaled and shook his head, continuing to rub his shoulder. "Actually, my dad died. I just have this viewing thing to go to on Monday."

Rick sobered instantly. "Aw man, RJ. I'm sorry. That was so stupid. I was just kidding about the dog." He babbled to excuse his joking.

RJ interrupted his boss. "Don't worry about it. The viewing is at night, but my sister will want me around that morning. I don't really want to leave her alone." He stopped to think. "Oh, and while we're talking about it, Jordan will need Monday off too. He's better with my sister than I am." RJ concluded, covering all of the bases as usual.

Feeling rather low, Rick agreed readily. "Sure, sure. RJ, I want you two to take Tuesday and Wednesday off as well." He paused, quieting his tone slightly. "My uncle passed away in July, so I know how that can be."

"Rick, all we need is Monday." RJ immediately frowned at the idea of having half a week with no work to do. He scratched his chin as he shook his head.

Rick's head was shaking as well, but being one of the few authorities above RJ, he put his foot down. "No. If you're so desperate for work, then you can take a few of the new alignment documents home with you. Look over the prints and make notes on any changes you think they need." Rick stopped talking and glanced over at the gold-framed picture of his family sitting on his desk. "I don't want to see you at work until Thursday. You know that you both have three bereavement days. I'm putting it on that." His tone was firm.

"Rick, I don't need to – " RJ persisted, nervous at being trapped in the apartment with his devastated sister.

"Take care of your mom or sister and spend some time with your family. I won't take no for an answer, and if either of you show your faces in here before Thursday, I'll fire you on the spot." Rick threw in his always-valid trump card, which closed RJ's mouth. He hung up the phone before RJ could muster up a persuasive argument, which was good, because all RJ could think to say was a weak, "But! But!"

Slamming the telephone receiver down in frustration, RJ frantically gathered up the papers for the new alignment policy and any sketches he could find and stuffed them into his black briefcase. It was five minutes after five o'clock when Jordan came by and opened his door. "Hey. Are you ready to go? I have to catch Rick before he leaves to ask him for Monday off." Jordan picked up RJ's jacket from off of the gold coat hanger and tossed it at him.

RJ shook his head as he caught his coat. "Don't bother. I already did. He said if we come back before Thursday next week, we're fired." He put his leather coat on and grabbed his briefcase. "Oh, and apparently we get three days of bereavement pay. Whatever that is." RJ shook his head. "You can work on the new alignment policy with me if you want to."

Jordan stood wide-eyed with his hand frozen on the door handle. "Man, RJ! What did you say to him?" He almost smiled. He knew that Isabel would need him, and that thought fulfilled him almost completely.

"Nothing. I just asked for Monday off for the viewing, and he gave us Tuesday and Wednesday off too. Magic touch, I guess." RJ kidded, lightening his mood a little.

They both went home and tried to be normal and carry out their daily tasks. Jordan went to the gym, and RJ attempted to bury himself in his work. His attempts fell short, because the phone did not stop ringing until after dark. Family and friends of the family called all day long, sending their condolences and love. RJ took all the calls with as much grace and sincerity as he could muster, allowing every caller to give their dime store psychology advice so that they felt they did their part. In truth, no one could help him. All of the well-wishes and spiritual phrases tossed his way only made him feel worse. After his work was interrupted for the thirteenth time, RJ unplugged the phone. Of all the times that he insisted on secluding himself from the world, this was the one time that actually felt justified. He reviewed the remainder of his work papers, and was interrupted only by thoughts of his dad.

After he'd decided that work was not serving its purpose of distracting him, RJ realized he needed something to keep himself busy. Dreading Isabel's arrival home motivated him to do chores he would not otherwise do. RJ picked up the damp blue dishrag that hung on the sink and began to hurriedly swipe at the already clean counter. Really, this task accomplished nothing, but it gave him purpose for at least eight and a half minutes, as he made sure all tables, chairs and countertops were spotless. When RJ had something to do, it kept his mind from wandering. Motion helped to soothe him. Isabel would argue with him when he would work too much overtime, insisting that he needed to deal with his demons instead of avoiding them. He knew that it was true, but he felt powerless when left alone with his terrible thoughts.

At 6:39 exactly, Geoff did his usual rat-a-tat-tat on RJ's apartment door, letting himself in after the last knock. Going into the kitchen to talk to RJ, Geoff dropped his backpack on the floor. "Hey man, Jordan told me about your dad." Geoff hugged RJ. As strange as guy-to-guy hugs usually look, hugs that came from Geoff always seemed to fit. They were safe and sincere, as was the friendship. As Geoff briefly held his friend, RJ held his breath to keep from talking or being relieved or feeling anything. The hug lasted five seconds. If Geoff would have held on for six, RJ may have been forced to exhale his pain.

Stretching out his shoulders, RJ returned to his faithfully silent rag. "Yeah." He spoke quietly. Not really knowing if he was sad that his dad died, or sad that his dad was the man that he was, or sad for his sister, or sad for the entire four years that their dad flipped out, or sad because, well, with this many conflicting thoughts, sad was the only emotion that seemed to surface itself. He was just... sad.

Being the overly empathetic friend, Geoff leaned his elbow on the counter, staring at RJ. Clearing his throat to bring RJ back to reality, Geoff spoke. "Jordan and I talked about it, and we decided that I would go with you to the viewing, and Jordan would stay with Isabel... whatever she decides to do. Is that okay?" Geoff asked, trying to take care of the situation with as few bumps as possible.

"Good. That's a great idea. Thanks. Tell Jordan 'thanks' too." RJ snapped back to life.

Geoff rolled his eyes and stood up straight. "Well, you know Jordan. Any chance to baby her, he'll jump at."

RJ halfway smiled. "Yeah, well, better him than me."

Grabbing the dishrag up off the counter, Geoff looked at RJ. "Hey, do you want to play Playstation?" He tossed the rag into the sink.

Finally, he had found something normal. "Yes!" RJ answered as if Playstation was the one ticket to his happiness. The two boys sat on the couch and played video games for two hours until Geoff's mind went numb. Eventually they called Jordan over for reinforcements, and Geoff took a nap on the Lazy Boy.

Unrelenting, they played until eight o'clock, when they heard Isabel's footsteps outside the door. It was the one sound that RJ had been dreading all day long.

Immediately the game went off and Geoff woke up as she entered the apartment.

Not knowing why, RJ's sadness for his sister came out as frustration and anger as she pranced through the silent apartment.

As she came out and asked what was wrong in that innocent tone of hers, RJ's anger grew. "Sit down, Eesa!" He finally barked.

Chapter Three

RJ searched for the right words to say to his sister. The look on her face told him that he was scaring her, which he knew would not help. Her young eyes stared up at him, concerned only for her brother's anger. He despised himself for being the one who would throw the distressing news onto her. Rubbing his stomach, RJ tried very hard not to look at her.

"Isabel, last night, um... dad had a heart attack." RJ finally got out the words. Each one he spoke aggravated his stomach more and more.

She looked up at him with her dark eyes. Then she glanced at Geoff on the Lazy Boy, who was anxiously leaned forward. *Such drama.* She thought, not really understanding the reason for their highly-strung angst.

"Last night, dad passed away." RJ finished, studying her reaction.

Her face was emotionless, suddenly glazed with stone. "Oh. Is that what all of this is about?" Isabel tossed her hair carelessly. "Are you okay, RJ?" Her face showed very little concern for her brother.

Floored by her non-reaction, RJ babbled. "Not really, but I'm more concerned about you. I guess I thought you'd be upset." He shrugged his tensed shoulders, his tone softening.

As if the tension could not get any thicker, Isabel looked right into his concerned eyes. "Why?" Icicles could have formed around her lips; her voice was emotionless and cold. Looking around the room at the boys, she almost chortled at their fear. "Why would I be upset? Why should he affect this family at all? Why?" Careful not to let even a hint of passion sneak into her voice, Isabel cleared her throat. "I know how close you two used to be. I am sorry your dad died, RJ." She tried to show sympathy, but refused to claim their father as her own. When all three boys stared at her incredulously, she added, "That's all I got."

Her sympathy was short-lived. "So who wants to go to Barney's?" She stood, lightly patting Jordan's shoulder.

RJ rubbed his forehead. "Eesa, stop it. You don't drink. We still have to talk about the funeral."

"Whose funeral?"

"Dad's funeral!" RJ almost shouted, not quite knowing how to handle his own sister. "For crying out loud! Your dad just died! We are not going to Barney's!" RJ began pacing.

"Fine. I'm going out. You can feel whatever you want about your dad, RJ. As much as he screwed up your life, I'm surprised that you're so upset about it. But he didn't *just* screw me up, RJ." Isabel stopped before she could raise her voice. Looking at her thumb for a moment, she calmed herself down. "Let's not get into this right now. Please." She shook her head and left for her room, quietly shutting the door behind her. Not really knowing what to do, her thought process stopped.

Inside the living room, the boys whispered quietly to each other, trying to decide what to do next. They finally agreed that Jordan should talk to

Isabel about the viewing, and Geoff and RJ would turn in for the night.

Geoff and RJ both left to sleep their troubled sleep, while Jordan summoned his courage and knocked on his friend's bedroom door.

Isabel still had not moved, and the knock snapped her to attention. "Come in." She consented, knowing that Jordan was the only one who would want to be with her right now.

Her friend opened the door and cautiously walked in, shutting it behind him. "Sweetie? I have to talk to you." He said, carefully wrapping his arms around her. He swayed her body gently from side to side, almost rocking her. Kissing her forehead absentmindedly, he continued. "Do you want to go to the viewing? There's no funeral service." He spoke calmly, still swaying.

"No." She answered straight. "I am not going. Please don't try to make me." Finally she convinced herself to relax in his arms, allowing her feel safe once again.

Jordan's eyebrows furrowed together, obviously concerned. "Of course I won't try to make you go. You can do whatever you want." He consoled her.

She nodded into his chest. "Okay. I think I want to go to bed, Jordan." She pulled away slowly.

"Okay, Bel. I'm here if you need me. You know that, right?" He felt desperate to remind her as he reached for the knob.

"Yeah. I know. I'm fine though." She said mindlessly. After he left, she immediately went to bed. It was barely nine o'clock, but she could not will her body to do anything but sleep.

At night, the apartment was dead silent. The only sound you could hear was RJ tossing and turning in bed. In the apartment across the hall,

Geoff slept like a rock, complete with a pool of drool dripping onto his pillow. Every so often he would snore for a few breaths, as he always did after a long day. Jordan slept with his arms folded across his chest like the brick wall he was, silencing the world. Quietly and slowly, the night filled both apartments.

A loud, blood-curdling scream shattered the silence like a bowling ball through a window. The scream jerked RJ to attention, though he had just managed to drift off to sleep. At first he thought it was a dream, but the second scream cleared up any confusion. The scream was real. It was Isabel's scream, and all too familiar to her brother.

Ice coursed through his veins and froze him to the core. *Isabel.* He panicked. A hundred flashbacks flooded his memory, clouding his mind from thinking clearly.

The next screams were even louder and more scared. Among the hellish screams, he made out her words.

"Stop! Help! Get away... from me! Dad! Please! RJ, stop him!" These horrible phrases were followed by more and more of the haunted screams and several cries for help.

This went on for a while until RJ could not take one more second. Running across the hall, he pounded on the boys' door with all his might. Geoff answered as quickly as he could jump out of bed, and Jordan followed behind sleepily, not bothering to put pajama bottoms over his boxers or don a shirt. When the door opened, RJ stumbled headfirst into the apartment, holding his stomach as though he were going to have a baby on their kitchen floor. "RJ, what the –" Geoff yawned.

"I can't hear this again! She's doing it again, and I can't make it stop!" RJ choked out, grabbing the flesh around his middle.

Jordan stood beside him, uncomfortably patting his back. "What is she doing? What can't you stop?" Jordan tried to fully wake up.

RJ held himself tighter. "She used to do this every night in high school. Every night! I can't hear her screams!" RJ shouted, still not able to calm down. "Her night things make me crazy!" Almost on his knees, RJ looked like a child.

Jordan and Geoff exchanged puzzled glances. Finally Geoff spoke, "Why don't you just wake her up?" He asked, shrugging his tired shoulders.

RJ took a few breaths and shook his head. "You can't wake her up in the middle of it. It's next to impossible to fully wake her up out of one. Even if I could, her shrink said that could be bad, because then she might remember what she was dreaming. If I just let her sleep through it, then in the morning she won't remember that she had one."

Jordan helped RJ to stand up straight. "Oh. Well that's not good for you. It's just nightmares?"

RJ looked at them incredulously, as though they had not heard him at all. "No! Not nightmares. They're called night terrors. They're worse than nightmares because they're real. They're not things your brain makes up, hers are real memories. Every night! I can't do this again!" RJ's stomach felt as though it was scratching against a cheese grater.

Geoff piped up. "Does she take any medicine for it?"

"She hasn't had one in years. Not since we moved out. She used to take some stuff, but we don't even keep it in the house anymore. I can't hear this all over again." RJ began to sweat. "I swear, I can't." RJ shook his head in pain.

"Well we'll have to take her in first thing tomorrow. I'll make her an appointment." Geoff instructed with his hands resting on his hips. "RJ, you take my bed tonight. I'll sleep in your room." Geoff left for his room to grab his pillow. Looking over his shoulder at the boys, he said, "She's twenty-five. She shouldn't be having these. Normally just children have night terrors, don't they?" He disappeared into his room.

Emerging with a pillow and alarm clock, Geoff sighed heavily. "You do know that she'll probably have to be evaluated by the psychiatrist. Also, I can look for some information on her night terrors. New medications maybe. I really don't know anything about them. We'll see. I'll talk to Dr. Taylor tomorrow." His sleep deprivation was beginning to take its toll as he tripped over his own foot.

RJ's shoulders relaxed ever so slightly. "Thanks, man. Are you sure you can handle sleeping over there?" RJ untucked his undershirt from his pajama pants, and then tucked the left side in again, getting out the last of his frazzled energy.

"I don't mind. I listen to people scream all day long. After a certain point, it just numbs you out." He smirked.

RJ looked at Geoff and Jordan with appreciation.

"Do you need anything from your place?" Geoff asked, scratching his head.

"No, man. Thanks." RJ's heart rate slowed as he made his way to Geoff's room and flopped onto the bed. He sat down on the nice bed in the quiet apartment. Geoff had green and blue striped flannel sheets, and mismatched orange pillowcases. Lucky for RJ, he had a few pictures of his sisters on his nightstand. Geoff had five older sisters who were all very attractive, and easy to think about as RJ drifted off to sleep, grateful for the silence.

Jordan reluctantly went back to bed as Geoff left for the dreaded apartment. Upon opening the door, he heard her terrible screams. He stood for a moment between RJ's room and hers. It was at that moment that he made an executive decision to go over RJ's head.

Boldly he opened Isabel's door. The naïve boldness melted into the floor when he saw her. Usually he saw her with her perfect hair in her perfect body, wearing her perfect smelling clothes. Not quite prepared for this, he momentarily forgot his mission. There she slept, not her usual beautiful ballerina sleep, but the sleep of something much darker. She was covered in sweat from head to toe. It was not the kind of sweat that surfaces only where the deodorant stick grazes, but instead it was a thick, visible sweat all over her body. Her hair was a swirling mass of black, matted and sticking to her sobbing face. Every time a scream erupted from her, she clawed the bed, leaving unnerving nail marks on either side of her.

The thing that scared him the most was her face. She looked terrified and angry and confused. Not just that, he soon realized, but she looked as though she were in physical pain. Immediately Geoff sprung into action. "Isabel, stop it! Wake up, honey. Wake up!" He tried to make himself heard over her yelling, though he was still very afraid. When yelling made no dent in her screams, he resorted to clumsily shaking her. This only terrified her more. Giving her another good shake and yelling to her, she reacted in a way he had not anticipated. She pushed him.

One would never guess that so much kinetic force could build up in one tiny person, but her shove flung him all the way back into the bedroom door. "Get off of me!" She screamed so hard that she choked a few times. "Dad! You're hurting me!"

Not knowing how to respond to this situation, he ran out of the apartment and went to wake Jordan.

"Jordan!" He whispered, verging on the edge of an emotional breaking point. He did not know if he was so upset because he had not slept in two days, or because he did not know how to help his sinking friend.

"Man! What?" Jordan was not exactly a bucket of sunshine when woken during twice in one night. He came out scratching his stomach.

"Help me." Geoff did his best to whisper quietly.

They both walked into the next apartment, Geoff running and Jordan stumbling. As soon as they entered, Jordan was taken aback by her screams. "What are we doing? Didn't RJ just say to leave her alone?" Jordan asked, still clad in only his boxers.

"Yeah. I just thought that if she did see how hard she was screaming that she would actually deal with this instead of pretending like it has nothing to do with her. Maybe she'll recognize that her dad actually died." Geoff stated his hypothesis, wringing out his hands.

Jordan shrugged. "Good enough. So what do you need me for?"

"I couldn't do it. I couldn't wake her up. She threw me across the room." He paused, letting the thoughts he was avoiding sink in. "I think she thought I was her dad." Speaking the words only upset him more. "I swear; I was just trying to wake her up." He pleaded with Jordan, assuming the worst of himself.

Softening a bit, Jordan put his rough hands on Geoff's shoulder. "Don't worry about it, man. She was asleep. You know she doesn't think you're like him." Taking a second to think, he got an idea. "Okay, hold on. I'll wake her up."

Walking to the kitchen, Jordan got out the big popcorn bowl and filled it with water.

Both boys went into her room, which had now become hot. Only Jordan inched toward her, and with a tortured look on his face, he poured the bowl of water on his treasure. "Help us all." He spoke quietly as she began to writhe under the stream of water.

Geoff thought that she looked like the fabled wicked witch melting under the flow of water. She twisted and screamed for a few seconds, and then she began to wake up.

Her eyes shot open like a deer in headlights, and the bitterly frantic cries for help turned into tears and confusion. Sitting up, she scrambled to the furthermost corner of the headboard. She cried deafeningly hard for about a minute until she began to calm herself down. Being the braver of the two, Jordan knelt on her bed. She was whimpering and still holding tight to the headboard, so Jordan waited a few more seconds before moving closer.

"Isabel," he spoke, "I'm going to hold you now. Is that alright?" He asked, displaying his hands to her to show his innocence.

Examining his hands in fear, she slowly nodded. Cautiously he wrapped his arms around her, making her start to whimper again. "Shh, doll. I've got you. You're safe now." He chanted the magic words as he rocked her back and forth.

"I don't know... what's happening. Why am I... why are you... I don't know!" She cried in tired exasperation.

Jordan just kept on rocking her, holding her head to his bare chest. "Shh... it's okay, honey. You just had a bad dream. It's okay now. I'm right here." He said as she clung tightly to his body.

Nodding and trying to let it all process, she whispered in his ear. "Please don't leave me. Please don't go." She wrapped her sweaty arms around his neck. "Please don't leave me."

Geoff had never felt so awful, and that included the time that he accidentally killed his sister Gloria's pet hamster. He wanted to be the one cradling his friend. He wanted to be the one to calm her down, not the one who reminded her of her father. Feeling so shameful that he could not lift his eyes to look at her, he finally spoke. "Isabel?"

At the sound of another voice in the room, she screamed and clawed at Jordan's neck.

"Shh, doll. Calm down. It's just Geoff." He rocked her. "You know, the only nurse who can grow facial hair." Jordan tried unsuccessfully to lighten the mood.

"Isabel, can I get you something to drink?" Geoff asked, bordering on tears again. His friend was afraid of him. Geoff was a very gentle man, and had never scared a woman with his presence. This thought sunk like a rock into the pit of his stomach and stayed there.

Isabel choked out her words. "Geoff?" She spoke. "Geoffrey, is that you?" Her voice sounded tiny, pained, and not like her own.

"Yeah, Bel. It's me. Are you okay?" In fear he tried to hold back any tears that were surfacing in his heart.

She cried softly. "I... I don't know. Why is everyone in my bedroom? I just want to go to sleep! I... I don't know what to do!" She sniffled into Jordan's shoulder.

Jordan looked over at Geoff and shook his head. "That's okay, Bel. You're going to sleep with me tonight." He positioned himself around her and picked her up, sliding to the end of the bed.

"But, but why can't I sleep in my bed?" She asked, getting groggier.

"Because your bed is soaked, my dear." Jordan grunted as he stood up, repositioning her tiny body in his arms.

"Oh, no." She closed her eyes, already falling back to sleep. Obviously Geoff's idea had not worked. RJ had been right.

As the bedraggled three entered into the boys' apartment, RJ awoke and came out. "What's going on?" He asked.

Jordan shot the sleepy brother a look that told RJ not to mess with him. "You can sleep in your room now, RJ. We'll see you in the morning." He spoke, casting authority over RJ. Not bothering to stick around for his rebuttal, Jordan retreated to his room with his friend. He kicked the door closed behind him to shut out the world.

He slowly and carefully laid her on his bed, giving her, of course, the good pillow. When he tried to pull away, she half awoke and began crying and shivering. "No!" She begged. "Please don't leave me!" She clung to his neck.

"Shh, shh. It's okay. I'm not going anywhere." He reassured her, kissing her warm forehead. He stood over the bed next to her, moving her over and tucking her in.

She clung to him with all of her tired might, forcing him to stand still. "Please don't leave me."

She continued to whisper, getting less frantic and more exhausted. "Don't let dad get me, RJ. Please don't... don't go." She grew drowsy and her grip on Jordan began to loosen.

Jordan stood still and kept watching her until he was sure she was asleep. Much too tired to process all of this emotion, he held his face in his tired hands. Trying to clear his mind, Jordan took the blanket off the foot of the bed to make a spot to sleep on the floor. He took the extra pillow off the bed, being careful not to wake the dead. Jordan could sleep anywhere, so the hardwood floor was just fine for him. Still, he tossed. He had known all about their dad. He had heard the horror stories and seen RJ's scars. He had even talked to their grandmother about it. Still, nothing had prepared him for her night terrors. Seeing her like that made him viciously protective of her. He made his temporary bed between her and the door, making sure that nothing could get to her that night.

Both Geoff and Jordan could not stop thinking about what had happened that night. Neither of them had ever known home lives like that. Jordan had grown up with his mother, and the only traumatic thing that had ever happened to him was that he never knew his father. Geoff's family was fully functional, and the worst family problem he had ever encountered was trying to keep his masculinity in a house full of women. Neither of the boys knew what to do in this situation, and that worried them even more.

Morning came earlier than usual for the three boys, and the moans and groans seemed to be the only language spoken as they each tumbled out of their respective rooms.

Isabel woke up feeling the same as she did every morning, except this time she was in a different bed. Yawning and stretching out her back, she wondered why she had fallen asleep in Jordan's room.

As she got out of the bed, she kept the blanket wrapped around her for warmth. The boys kept their apartment colder than hers, so she kept tight inside the blanket as she opened the bedroom door. Finding the apartment empty, she scooted across the hall to find all three men awake and eating breakfast. Geoff was making eggs and French toast before he went to the hospital, and the two engineers were eating greedily at the counter. The syrup was parked by RJ, who liked to pour a little droplet of syrup on each individual bite before he put it in his mouth.

When they saw Isabel, Geoff put his spatula down and wrapped her in a long hug. "I love you so much, Bel. Are you okay?" He rubbed her lower back with his thumb.

Shrugging her shoulders at his strange greeting, she allowed herself to sink into the hug. "I love you too, Geoff. I'm just fine. Are you okay?" She gave him a look as she finally pulled away.

"I told you." RJ shook his head as he stuffed his mouth with a forkful of eggs. "How'd you sleep, Bel?" He almost smiled.

"Good. I just have one question. Why did I sleep in your bed, Jordan? I don't even remember going over to your place last night." She walked over to Jordan, and he pulled her onto his lap.

Jordan kissed her shoulder as he continued to eat. "I think the bigger question is, why are you wearing my blanket?" He teased, holding a piece of French toast to her mouth.

Isabel rolled her neck. "No thanks. I'm not hungry. And your apartment is like sixty-five degrees, so it was either the blanket or frostbite."

Geoff shook his head disapprovingly. "You don't want breakfast? You always eat when I cook." He gestured with the spatula in his hand.

Isabel yawned loudly, forgetting to cover her mouth. "I know. Just let me wake up. I'm sure I'll be hungry later."

"Eesa, honey, we need to talk to you." Jordan tugged on her stubbornly wavy strands of hair.

"Sure." She stood up and went over to the refrigerator, blanket and all. "If it's about Dad, then forget it."

"It's not about Dad. Last night you had a night terror." Jordan stated as a matter of fact. All tact had left him after a fitful night's sleep on the hardwood floor.

Isabel froze. "What?" Suddenly embarrassed, she did not turn to look at them. Blood rushed to her cheeks, turning them a deep red. "I'm sorry, RJ. Did I wake you up?" She reached into the half-empty fridge for the jar of strawberry jam.

"Eesa, Geoff got you an appointment with Dr. Taylor for ten o'clock today. Hopefully he can write you a prescription. You'll probably just take what you were on before." RJ explained with a mouthful of French toast.

Isabel just stood for a moment, letting it all sink in. She unscrewed the jar and took a spoon from the drawer. Dipping the spoon in and putting the jam in her mouth calmed her nerves a bit as she continued her conversation with the boys. "Okay guys, I'm fine with whatever you want me to do today, but I was never on any medication for my night terrors. You don't take anything for those." She licked her spoon, and then she went for another dip in the jar.

RJ's eyebrows furrowed together. "Yes, you did. The little round pink pills you had to take." He scratched his face involuntarily.

"Those were my birth control. You don't take anything for night terrors. They just go away on their own." She explained, deflating the air out of their brilliant plan.

RJ pushed the last few pieces of French toast around on his plate. "Why would you need birth control? You can't have... you know." RJ looked down, feeling rather low for bringing up the subject.

Isabel inhaled slowly, trying to avoid thinking about the white elephant tiptoeing around the room. "It was before the second abortion, RJ. When I actually needed it."

No one spoke for several minutes. RJ's mouth turned into a frown and his mood flattened almost to the floor. "Great." He tapped his fork on his glass of orange juice. "I guess you can cancel those appointments, Geoff. I'm sorry." RJ sighed as his mind went back to square one.

Geoff stared at his blanket-clad friend in disgust. "Isabel, that is so gross. I can't handle watching you eat that right out of the jar." Geoff shivered as his eyes followed her. "I mean, at least put it on toast or something. That's just sick."

All she could do was try to find her smile. "But it is *so* good like this. Don't you ever get cravings like that? Where you just have to have something that second?" She took another mouthful of red, sticky jam.

"Yeah, but why can't you crave something normal, like chocolate or cookies? Jam? Plain? That is so gross!" He grimaced, washing out the pans he had used for breakfast.

Isabel rolled her eyes and went into the living room. "Please." She dismissed his complaint.

Jordan slammed his fork down and swiveled his stool around to face her. "Geoff! You are so wrong!" He exclaimed in his most feminine voice, fingers spread out and flailing around in the air. Standing up, he walked into the living room in full strut. He tried to make Isabel smile by doing a quick attempt at a ballet jump. He landed with a thud on the carpet and took the jar from her, displaying it in his best Vanna White fashion. The audience oo'd and awed accordingly. "Why Geoff, can't you see the nutritional value just oozing out of this jar?" He did a quick twirl to keep it out of Isabel's anxious grasp.

"Jordan! Man, you think you are so funny!" She did her best not to smile as she jumped for the much-desired jar.

Jordan was holding the coveted jar just out of her reach. No matter how high you can jump, five feet and five inches tall is no match for six feet and three inches. Jordan put his whole hand over her face to keep her from jumping. "Um, excuse me." He cocked his hip to the side. "I am trying to tell our audience about the miracle product. Do you mind?" Jordan huffed a prissy huff and continued, holding his product high. "Not only does this miracle jam contain two of the basic core food groups (fruit and sugar), but there is an added feature that sets our miracle jam apart from the jams of yester-year. Geoff, tell our studio audience about the added feature." Jordan gestured for Geoff to join him, and like the entertainer that he was, Geoff came running up to the makeshift stage.

Geoff put on the phoniest smile that he could muster and took out his game show host voice. This was all to the amusement of RJ, and now Isabel, who were watching with delight. "Well Vanna, not only does this satisfy a half serving of fruit and four servings of sugar, but when used properly, can cause your facial hair to grow three times faster than normal. Fellas, does your lady complain that you are too baby-faced? Does she laugh at your hard-earned peach fuzz? Well just two spoonfuls of this miracle jam every morning could leave you looking like this!" Geoff waved for RJ to come "on stage".

RJ rolled his eyes like the control freak he was, but still joined in. This much fun was too difficult to resist. He reluctantly stood, trying to hide his embarrassed smile. "I've been on the miracle jam plan for only two weeks now, and I've already grown this manly stubble." RJ flexed for effect.

Geoff pretended to swoon and gasped. Then, in his cheesiest game show host voice he wiped the imaginary sweat off of his forehead. "Whoa, stud! Put those pythons away!" He said, now sporting an imaginary microphone.

Isabel was now curled over on the couch, laughing and hooting. Jordan loved to make her laugh. This little ball of giggle poured out of her throat like honey, and oozed itself all over his heart. He could not help but love her.

All three would-be comedians gave in to the infectious laughter, joining hands to take a bow. Isabel clapped and shouted their praises as Jordan leaned over to feed her a spoonful of the coveted miracle jam, dripping a little on his own hand. Isabel looked up at his smile and continued giggling as she swallowed the only food she wanted. *Such silliness*, she thought as she leaned forward and licked the stray red blob off of Jordan's hand. Jordan froze as his body temperature rose two degrees.

"Awe, gross Bel!" Geoff covered his eyes with his hand.

RJ piped up, "What?" He sat down in his Lazy Boy.

"Eesa licked Jordan!" Geoff cried, scrunching his nose. Working in a medical facility made Geoff extremely bacteria-conscious.

"Anywhere interesting?" RJ teased, smacking Jordan's rear end.

Jordan jumped, standing straight up. Slowly, he smiled again, taking a seat next to Isabel on the couch. Holding her hand and kissing it affectionately, he handed over the miracle jam. "Here you go, honey. Don't make yourself sick." He said as she cuddled into him, happily enjoying her strawberry jam. Whenever she snuggled to him, it would make his chest swell with manly pride. His chin lifted a good three inches, and his back lengthened to lift his shoulders as tall as they could get.

Geoff walked over to the kitchen, putting the remainder of the dirty dishes in the sink as he tried to put their blatant flirtation out of his mind. "Okay, young lovers. I've got to go to work now." He paused for effect. Upon hearing no pity from his friends, Geoff continued. "No, no. No sympathy, please. I enjoy being the only one of us who works Saturdays."

RJ droned in complete monotone. "Oh, poor baby. The inhumanity. I am outraged." He spoke flatly while surveying the room for the remote control. When he finally spotted it, he spoke up. "But before you go, could you grab the remote for me? It's on top of the TV." RJ bordered on whining.

Halfway out the door, Geoff rolled his eyes. "Yeah, I'll get right on that. Hey, while you're waiting you can hold your breath and wait for those pigs to fly." He exited with his sarcasm obviously still in tact.

Huffing in defeat, RJ looked over at the two couch potatoes. "Jordan, I think the game's on. Would you get me the remote?"

Jordan shook his head. "No way, man. I've got a beautiful woman curled up at my side. Ain't nothing moving me off this couch." He closed his eyes and leaned his head back into the couch. Isabel sat, unaffected by the compliment. All she wanted was to eat her precious strawberry jam. She couldn't explain it, but something was strange inside of her, and the answer to her unknown problem was somewhere inside the jar of jam. She ate and ate, not feeling full or sick, just searching for the missing puzzle piece, though not really knowing what was missing.

"Eesa?" RJ begged, dreading getting off of his appropriately named "Lazy Boy".

"I can't." She stated flatly, making sure not to break concentration with her jam. "Aliens took over my body, and well, they don't like you." She looked up at him, faking innocence.

RJ smiled obnoxiously at her and mimed a quick laugh. "Fine. I guess I'll do all the work, as usual." He jeered, sour at having to get up.

A loud guffaw escaped from Isabel's mouth. "Excuse me? You? What is this alleged 'work' that you do so much of around here?" The spoon clicked itself against her teeth as she ingested the last mouthful without even realizing it.

RJ stood indignantly. "Maybe you didn't see the counter that I cleaned yesterday." He reached for the remote control.

Covering her mouth with her hand, Isabel awed in mock astonishment. "Forgive me, Mr. Clean. I totally forgot. That one act of selfless cleanliness breaks your whole track record of not cleaning anything. You poor thing. Sit down; you must be exhausted." She teased, clinking the spoon in the bottom of the jar and pulling it out empty. Taken aback, she looked down at her empty spoon. *Gone? How could it be gone?* She thought to herself sadly. *Time to open another jar!* She sang in her head happily. She loved being the first person to dip her spoon into a fresh jar of jam.

"So funny!" RJ sat back down in his chair, flipping to find the best game.

"I'll be right back." She said to Jordan and left for the kitchen in hot pursuit of another jar of strawberry jam.

Jordan stared at the television, already feeling cold where she had been next to him. "Sure you'll come back." He rolled his neck from side to side, cracking it just for the satisfaction of the crunch. "They always come back."

Searching the cabinet where she kept the reserve preserves, Isabel found only six jars left. She made her own jam and canned it herself. There was something about canning her homemade goodness that made her feel like a mother, a good mother even. Her last canning day had produced fifteen jars of the delicious strawberry jam. Seeing only six made her a little sad, only because she wished for a whole cabinet stocked full of the red jam. Pulling a jar out, she took a moment to look in the cabinet again. Now there were only five jars.

Rejoining the two vegetables in the living room, Isabel cuddled up to Jordan again. As she cozied herself into his outstretched arm, she opened the new jar with the edge of the spoon, making a loud *pop*. Jordan's face contorted and his body recoiled slightly. "Oh my gosh, Eesa! That is so gross! Did you seriously finish that entire jar?" Even RJ looked up from his football daze.

“The jar was practically empty, Jordan. Don’t freak out.” She shoveled another heaping spoonful into her mouth bashfully.

“Liar!” Jordan cried, pointing an accusatory finger at her face. “That jar was half full! You ate half a jar of jam in one sitting, you sick, sick woman! And now you’re starting on a new one?” Jordan shook his head disapprovingly. “That is so disgusting, Isabel. I mean, I’m nauseous just thinking about it.”

Rolling her eyes, she exclaimed, “You are over exaggerating, and you sound like a woman, too.” She threw the insult in because she knew that he was right.

Saturday came and went with barely any notable conversation or confrontations. Saturday night proved to be equally as horrifying as Friday night, and Sunday morning found Geoff sleeping in and the other three musketeers back on the same comfortable couch.

The three adults sat like children, glued to the television for two whole hours. RJ, reclined in his Lazy Boy, watched every play and even tried to predict some of the downs. Though he would never voice his predictions to his fellow couch potatoes, he found joy in the smugness he felt when his silent predictions were accurate. He loved watching football almost as much as he liked playing it. The aggressive sport really connected with him. The tossing of huge bodies through the air satisfied his need for testosterone, and always kept him interested.

Jordan, on the other hand, could not have been less enthused. His focus this particular morning was not on the football game, but on something greater. His left hand strummed on the couch nervously, and inside of his medium-sized lips, his teeth ground together in concern. Last night had been one of the worst nights he had suffered through in a long time. Not because he had been woken up, or because he had slept on the hard floor for two nights now (although, those two factors did contribute to his dismal disposition), but because he did not know what to do about Isabel. The feeling of helplessness sat on his shoulders, and curled itself around his neck. His fingers itched to hold something that had once felt to him like an extension of his hand. He had not had an urge this strong since he had quit smoking for good, and right now a cigarette was all he wanted. It had been a year since he had quit, and to this day it was the worst thing he ever had to go through in his adult life. Over time, his cravings had still been haunting, but manageable. However, watching bad things happening to good people really got under his skin. With Isabel burrowed into his side, the temptation was almost unbearable. For the first time in a long time, he needed to smoke... now.

Around the cool of noon, the doorbell buzzed, breaking RJ out of his second hour of football. Jordan sprang off the couch, knocking Isabel to the floor. The kinetic energy it took to calm the craving was too intense for him. “Oh, I’m sorry, Bel.” He helped her up, recalling a bit of shaken tenderness.

Isabel’s forehead wrinkled. “You okay?” She was always the first to notice changes in her friend. He was never that careless with her.

He did not even hear her as he dashed to the door. He pushed the intercom button. “Yeah?”

Jordan asked with the taste of the sweet nicotine on his mind.

"Is that my grandson? I've come to see my grandchildren." Came the tiny Italian voice.

A smile swept over Jordan's face as he momentarily forgot about his coveted cigarette. "Come on up, Grandma." He buzzed his adopted grandmother into the building.

"Oh, I have to change out of my pajamas before we have company. RJ, did you know that Grandma was coming over?" Isabel hopped up and scampered into her bedroom.

RJ shrugged, getting back into the game. Jordan subtly walked back into the living room and turned the television off. "Grandma's on her way up." Jordan announced.

"Okay, I'm up." RJ stood with a groan.

"She's so great to come over. Man, she loves you two." Jordan stopped to pick one of the throw pillows off the floor. "I don't remember the last time my grandma came over just to say 'hi' to me for no reason." Jordan stretched and scratched his stomach. "Shoot, I can't remember the last time my mom called me."

RJ saw Jordan stretching and realized that his back felt a bit stiff. Stretching and guffawing at the same time, RJ rolled his eyes. "Right. She never comes by for no reason. She always has a mission."

A little tiny knock sounded at the front door. Jordan bounced over and flung the door open. What he expected was one shriveled grandmother, possibly accompanied by a hunched grandfather. What he got was a shriveled grandmother, a hunched grandfather, and a whole slew of towering Italians. "Oh, wow. Come on in, everybody. We didn't expect company." That was all he could stutter as the mafia-looking family walked in, twenty strong.

Grandma was armed with lasagna, and was accompanied by several aunts and cousins bearing various casseroles. Within no more than fifteen seconds, the apartment had been changed from the only noise in the room being the television, to there being so much talking that you could not even hear the sportscaster. The counter went from clean and empty to completely loaded with delicious aromas of food.

They all shifted like an anthill containing too many ants around the small apartment. Everyone made sure to hug, kiss and pinch the two boys. When Isabel emerged, the flock started all over again. Loud Italians never run out of things to talk about, and even two days before burying someone, there was still plenty of affection and funny stories to exchange.

Isabel's first hug came from her Aunt Nina, who happened to be her favorite aunt. Aunt Nina was a rather large and busty woman, and her hugs always came from her heart. One hug from Aunt Nina usually squeezed all of Isabel's emotions to the surface like a toothpaste tube on its first squirt. They would have amazing talks that lasted for hours. Of all the women in her life, she felt most intimate with Aunt Nina. This time when she hugged her niece, it felt very different to Nina. This hug did not surface anything in Isabel but a shallow smile and empty eyes. Aunt Nina hugged a little tighter, waiting to feel her favorite niece sag in her embrace. Isabel hugged her back, unaffected by the love. "Isabella, how are you, dear?" She asked, more concerned by her non-reaction than by an insane outburst.

"Just fine, Aunt Nina. How are you?" She replied, gently pulling away. From that hug she was swooped away into dozens more hugs, leaving Nina speechlessly sad.

Everyone was swept up in the enchantment of just being together except for one person who clung to the far corner of the kitchen. Although she tried to disappear into the background, her attempts fell short. The only fair-skinned blonde stood out like a blinking light in the room stuffed with olive-skinned, dark-haired Italians. She stood, rifling through the napkin basket on the counter so that she would appear to be busy.

"RJ! How are you doing?" Grandpa pinched RJ's cheeks. Only cute little Grandpa, the most respected man in the family, could get away with pinching RJ's cheeks. Although the aged man almost always looked joyful, today he had a special spark in his eyes. This seemed unusual to RJ, seeing as how the funeral of the man's son-in-law was on Monday.

Hugging his grandfather, RJ almost smiled. It felt good to have a respectable father figure hug him. He made sure not to bend into the hug though, but to let it bounce off of his body so that he would not actually feel the full impact of his grandfather's love. "We're just fine, Grandpa." RJ answered for the household. "We weren't expecting the family. Is everything okay?" He asked, still not sure of that sparkle in his Grandpa's eye.

The elderly man patted RJ's stomach. "Do I need a reason to visit my favorite grandson? Tell you what, your family loves you. That's the reason." He smiled and tilted his head back, as if it was the best thing he had thought of all day.

"Hey! Hey! Why isn't the game on?" Cousin Tony hollered into the crowd. "Is this the wrong apartment? Because RJ never misses a game."

"Well, turn it on!" RJ shouted above the commotion, making his way to the kitchen to call

Geoff. Every step he took was halted by either a hug or a half dozen kisses, so it took several minutes to reach his destination. "Excuse me, Carrie." He picked up his little cousin off of the counter, passing her a faint smile on the way down. "I need the telephone." RJ awkwardly indulged his pint-sized cousin with as much affection as he could gather. Quickly disregarding the smile given to the chubby-fingered girl, RJ picked up the telephone and speed-dialed Geoff's number.

"Yeah?" Geoff asked. The boys used caller ID, so Geoff knew it had to be one of the two siblings.

"Hey, you want to wake up before noon and come over? The whole family's here and we've got food. Are you hungry?" RJ scratched the back of his head, shifting his weight to his other foot. As he turned that quarter inch, something bright caught his eye.

"Yeah, sure. Let me take a shower, I'll be over in a few. Did Marianna make her ravioli?" Geoff asked, still waking up.

"We've got every kind of food with pasta on this counter right now. Get clean and come help us eat, man." RJ hung up the phone and turned towards the counter to see what it was that had caught his eye.

The beautiful blonde woman stood in the corner of the kitchen, looking down at the spatula she twisted nervously in her hands. RJ had never fully appreciated hair that golden. It hung around her face in perfectly formed curls, teasing down to the tips of her shoulders. Though he was only a few feet from her, he felt as though he were watching her through a glass-paned window.

She seemed not to notice him staring at her, and kept fiddling with the spatula, pretending to be preoccupied. After several moments of RJ staring at this woman, he disregarded his personality and spoke. "Hi." He held out his hand with a boldness that surprised even him. "I'm RJ." He swallowed, hand still extended to this shy stranger. "That stands for Richard Joseph. My father's name was Richard, and Joseph because my parents were Catholic." RJ had not pieced together this many consecutive sentences in years (unless, of course, it involved his work). Like a runaway train, he just kept going. "I'm not Catholic." He felt a pressing need to clear that up. "I mean, I'm not anything. Well, I am something. I'm an engineer. I just don't like God." RJ was visibly sweating. "What I mean to say is that I don't go to a church. I don't really know anything about God, so I guess it's not fair for me to say that I don't like him. I just don't want to... um, so, yeah." RJ's forehead wrinkled in frustration as he licked his lips nervously, actively hating himself.

All that the bewildered blue-eyed doe could do was look at him and blush, trying to understand why this handsome man was rambling to her, of all people. She was trying to help him find some sort of ground level to come down to in order to help soothe him. It was obvious to her that he was Gina's cousin whose father had passed away. She and Gina had made plans to go to lunch that day, but their lunch was postponed so that Gina could go be with her family. Being the good friend that she was, the young woman offered to go along with her friend for emotional support.

"So no, I'm not Catholic." RJ concluded his almost conversation. His hand was still extended, because the lady had not taken his hand yet, for fear of interrupting this obviously troubled man.

She had compassion on him and slowly took his hand, nodding gently. "I'm Adela. I came with Gina... your cousin?" She assumed. Shrugging nervously, she twisted the spatula she had been clenching by her side. "She asked me to come with her to meet her family. I hope that my being here isn't at all inappropriate." She stared up at him with a worried expression.

RJ's eyes grew wide. "Oh no, no. We just weren't expecting the family to come over. You're very welcome here. Forget about it." He stuck his free hand in his pocket. "I'm glad that Gina brought you." He revealed, still in disbelief at his behavior. Catching his mistakes, he shook his head at himself. "I'm sorry. I'm making you uncomfortable. I'm an idiot. I'm sorry." Turning crimson red, he quickly turned and started walking away from her, hoping that the earth would open up and swallow him into the ground.

"Wait, RJ!" She raised her voice and reached out to touch his arm. The simple touch froze him. Embarrassed, he turned to face her. Now that she had his attention, she did not know what to do. She had felt so out of place there that the random conversation was actually a refreshing change for her. She stood, mentally grappling for something, *anything* to say, and finally she blurted out, "I'm not Catholic either." Hoping that this left field comment would convey her empathy toward him, she kept her hand on his arm. "I'm a Christian, but I'm not Catholic. I go to Blessed Faith Church downtown." He seemed to relax slightly, so she threw out some more tidbits. "I'm a Sunday school teacher for fourth and fifth grade girls. Um, this week we're learning about Jonah." She was surprised at how fast the words came babbling out of her mouth.

"Who's Jonah?" RJ looked interested, relieved that she had not yet run away screaming.

Adela was caught off guard. In her circle, everyone knew the Bible story about Jonah and the whale. "Jonah was a prophet of God in the Old Testament who tried to run from God. So to get his attention, God had a whale swallow Jonah. He was in the whale for three days and then he was spat out and given a second chance. Instead of running again, he chose to do what God had commanded him to do in the first place, which was to minister to the people of Nineveh." She summed up a half hour's worth of Bible lesson in a few sentences. Suddenly remembering what RJ had just expressed about God, she covered her mouth. "I'm sorry. We don't have to talk about that. I don't mean to be insensitive." She touched his arm again and let it remain there. She shook her head at herself. "You don't want to hear about Sunday school. You're probably thinking about Gina's uncle. He was your dad, right?"

RJ was taken with Adela. He had not been this captivated by anything besides work or the television in years, so talking about Jonah did not make him defensive in the least bit. Realizing for the first time in the conversation that she was a little insecure as well, he began to breathe easier. He almost smiled at her shy manor. Putting his hand over hers, he felt instantly warm from head to toe. "I don't mind hearing about Jonah. I'm sure you're a great Sunday school teacher, Adela." Saying her name brought the warmth through his body all over again. They looked at each other for a solid five seconds until Adela bashfully looked away.

A rough pair of hands slapped RJ on the back. "Hey, man. Who's your friend?" Jordan inquired, turning politely to Adela.

"Oh, man. Do you know anybody here?" RJ asked her, finally remembering his manners.

She shook her head. "I met some of them on the way here, but I don't remember anyone except for the grandparents, Gina and you. There are just so many of you!" She smiled, blushing.

Temporarily lost in the brightness of her smile, RJ hesitated. After a few seconds, he turned to Jordan. "This is our neighbor, Jordan. He and Geoff live across the hallway. Geoff is our other friend."

Jordan nodded politely and smiled, not extending his hand to her for fear that she would remove her hand from RJ's arm to shake his hand. Jordan was stunned at the whole scene. He had never seen RJ be interested in a conversation with really anyone other than them, and even that was rare. He looked sensitive, almost tender, holding onto her hand so gently. Jordan was practically speechless.

Adela smiled back. "It's nice to meet you, Jordan. I'm Gina's friend."

Still taken aback at RJ's behavior, Jordan stared at him in bewilderment. "Oh!" He turned back to the young woman, "Have you met Isabel?"

Confused as to whom she had already hugged and been greeted by, she bit her lip. "I don't think so. Is she one of Gina's cousins?"

"Yeah. She's RJ's sister, and she lives here too. Hold on, let me get her." Jordan jogged away to find his friend in the crowd. When he left, RJ leaned in towards Adela to reveal a secret thought that he had never really discussed with anyone before. Almost whispering by her ear, he said, "We've all been friends for years, but I think Jordan's in love with my sister. I don't think there was ever a time when he wasn't." RJ felt free to tell Adela things that the four of them would never talk about. She gave him a playful smile at this news that was really irrelevant to her. Just the same, she took the information as a coveted secret and gave his arm a light squeeze.

"Really?" She showed off her perfectly white teeth. "Well, he seems very nice. Do we want him to date her someday?" She felt privileged to be in on the secret.

RJ smiled back at her and quickly nodded. "Yeah, but Geoff and I just pretend to not see it. Watch them, you'll see it too. Oh, but don't tease them about it. They get really sensitive." RJ finished briefing her just as the two platonic lovebirds came bounding towards them. Adela was very glad to receive this information. She was beginning to feel almost comfortable with RJ now, and had still not removed her hand from his arm.

"Hi. I'm Isabel, RJ's sister. We're so glad that you could come visit us." Isabel beamed at Adela. She had not seen her brother willingly make physical contact with a woman in so long. He looked foreign to her, touching another person on his own free will. "Are you Aunt Nina's friend?"

Adela shook her head, still smiling at having someone to talk to. "No. I came with Gina. She insisted that I come today. I hope it's okay that I'm here." Even as she spoke, both Jordan and Isabel could not believe how perfect she was. She looked completely pure. Her perfect blonde hair hung in solid curls at her shoulders, while her snow-white skin made her stand out in the crowd. Her clean smile seemed natural. Everything about her looked respectable and feminine. Her rosy pink dress hung down past her knees, while a powdery lavender sweater covered her shoulders and arms. She looked like a porcelain doll on RJ's arm.

Breaking out of her stare, Isabel smiled. "It's great that you're here. Um, would you like to help me organize all the food on the counter?" Adela was glad to be able to help. She had felt so out of place before RJ had come over to her. She liked Isabel immediately.

"Yes. Please let me do something. I feel so useless." Adela smiled. "What can I do?" She turned to face the overflowing counter.

RJ found her enthusiasm endearing. Only for the sake of impressing her, RJ suddenly wanted to help too. Usually he was content with relying on Isabel to do everything. Something about the beautiful woman compelled him to participate in the life going on around him. "Yeah, can I help?" He spoke up, ignoring the looks he knew were coming.

Jordan and Isabel stared at him as though he had just started speaking in another language. "Sure, RJ. Why don't you and Adela put all the main dishes right here," she pointed to one side of the counter, "and the side dishes on this end." She walked to the end of the counter. "Put out the drinks and plates and stuff on this counter." She patted the small counter space by the sink. "I guess just put out whatever we have in the fridge to drink." Isabel instructed.

Jordan spoke up, "Geoff just bought a couple of two liters yesterday, and we've got all the paper plates and cups at our place."

"Okay. I'll help you bring them over." Isabel and Jordan scampered into the hallway, leaving the two love-struck adults to flirt like children while organizing the food.

As soon as the door shut behind her, Isabel squealed. "Oh my gosh! What was that?" She hopped from foot to foot, smiling with sheer glee. "Does he know her? I mean, I've never seen her before, have you?"

Jordan hopped up and down with her, unable to resist her joy. "No, he just met her here. Isn't she nice? I mean, she's so wide-eyed and sweet looking.

I've never seen him volunteer to help with anything! Did you see that?" They continued hopping for a few seconds until the boys' apartment door opened and Geoff breezed out.

Taking a step back at the sight of Jordan and Isabel hopping around the hallway, Geoff held his hands up to calm them down. "Whoa. What's wrong with you guys?" He tried not to smile.

Realizing that he had just been jumping for joy, Jordan became a little self-conscious and planted his feet firmly on the floor. "You will never guess what is happening in that apartment, Geoff." Jordan stood in front of the door, blocking Geoff's entrance. "RJ is acting like a human being!" Isabel was still hopping from all of the excitement.

Geoff raised one eyebrow at his roommate, who was acting even stranger than usual. "Okay, define 'human being'. I mean, is he smiling at people, or has Isabel finally taught him how to chew with his mouth closed?" He joked, smoothing out his green shirt. Getting distracted by his little friend bouncing up and down, Geoff grabbed her sides and tickled her.

"No!" She squealed. "It's a girl! Gina brought a girl friend, and RJ is totally smitten with her. Go see for yourself!" She pretended to kick Geoff on his backside to shoo him into the crowded apartment.

Opening the door, Jordan let Geoff into the overstuffed apartment and shut the door behind him. "Okay, let's go get the paper plates and stuff." He opened his apartment door and trotted to the kitchen.

Isabel began to think about what Adela would mean if she stuck around RJ long enough. "Hey Jordan, do you think that RJ will start dating her?" Isabel asked, trailing behind him.

"I hope so." He fished though the tall cupboard for the utensils. "Your brother has not been with a woman since high school. I think it's great that he's showing interest in the opposite sex again. Maybe she'll get him out of the apartment once in a while and he'll start having a life. That would be nice." He pulled out the utensils and set them on the counter. The napkins and paper plates were stored next to the fridge, so Isabel grabbed both stacks. "Hey." Jordan located the cups and gathered everything into his long arms. "You've got something on your face." He warned her.

Wiping her cheek on her shoulder, Isabel squirmed. "What? Get it off." She bordered on whining as they walked to the door, fully loaded with the much needed paper and plastic products.

Instead of putting his hand to her face, he bent down and kissed her cheek softly. She loved the way that he smelled, and used the opportunity to fill her senses with his spicy aftershave.

As he leaned to kiss her other cheek, the longing hit him once again out of nowhere. He urgently needed to smoke, and could not dismiss his craving. They walked over to the apartment across the hallway and handed their armloads to RJ and Adela. The food was all perfectly organized and ready to be eaten, thanks mostly to Adela. Jordan rested his hand on Isabel's back as he tried to speak low enough for only her to hear. "I'll be right back, Bel."

His touch sent an involuntary chill through her, but she tried to ignore it. She turned to face him, leaning her hip on the side of the counter. "Sure, Jordan. Are you going to get more pop?" She asked, ready to assign him the job.

Reaching for the knob, he realized that he had forgotten an alibi. "Yeah. I was going to hit the party store by your coffee shop." He lied, reopening the door.

"Oh, good. Hey, I'll go with you. I should really bring Homeless Joe something. I didn't get to see him yesterday. He's probably hungry." Isabel grabbed a plate and started filling it up with the hot food.

"No!" Jordan protested a little too quickly.

"Hey, Jordan!" Cousin Tony called, slapping him on the back and grabbing a plate.

Jordan nodded and smiled at Tony. "Hey, man." He turned his focus back to Isabel. "I mean, no. You shouldn't have to leave your family. I'll run it down to him and pick up the pop." He reached for a suitable explanation, hoping it would give him ten minutes to slip away.

Noticing his strange behavior, Isabel cocked her head to the side. "Okay, Jordan. If you want to." She narrowed her eyes, still observing him. "You remember where he sits, right? He's on the sidewalk a block down from the coffee shop. He usually sits by the lamppost. Oh, and he doesn't really talk, so don't be put off if he doesn't say thank you." She pulled out the aluminum foil and covered the plate. "Here you go." She handed the food to him. "Thanks."

Taking the plate, he checked for his wallet and exited as quickly as he could. The craving was getting more intense, and as he ran down the stairs he could feel the blood pumping hot in his ears. Though it was only a few blocks to the party store, he felt as though his nerves would shatter if he did not have satisfaction soon.

Upon reaching his destination, he flung open the door with his free hand, jumping at the jingle that the bell on the door made. He wasted no time at all grabbing any two-liter of pop, not caring to see which one his shaking hand landed on. He walked straight to the counter, picking out a blue lighter.

"Hey! How's my favorite nonsmoker?" The semi-familiar girl behind the counter perked up, setting down her Vogue magazine.

Smiling with a tinge of guilt, he slapped down his money, the pop, and the lighter. "Camel Straights." He requested, not quite able to recall her name. Unfortunately her nametag read "Baby Star", which did not help him much.

"I guess I spoke too soon." She pulled the cigarettes out from the rack behind her, taking his ten and ringing up the small purchase. "Bad day?" She tried to empathize with him, though realizing that she could not recall his name either.

"Not for me." Jordan took his change and put his purchase in his pocket. "Thanks." He made eye contact before leaving.

The coffee shop was only a short walk down the street, so Jordan jogged quickly to Homeless Joe. There he was, sitting by the lamppost just as Isabel had said he would be. He was slumped against the post, holding his cane.

"Hello, sir?" Jordan sat down beside him. "I'm Isabel's friend." He explained to the troubled man. Homeless Joe did not often get visitors aside from Isabel, so he did not quite know what to do.

Jordan stared at Homeless Joe, expecting some sort of a facial response. Joe did not speak or move the muscles in his face, but rather he looked back at the stranger, trying to decide if he was friendly or not. "My name is Jordan, and I live in Isabel's apartment building. She's my friend." He paused, feeling a little silly conversing with this man who was obviously not going to talk back. Jordan began to wonder if he had located the right "Homeless Joe". Looking around and seeing no other men sitting on the sidewalk, he continued explaining himself to who he hoped was the right man. "She's at the apartment today and asked me to run this out to you." He handed the man the aluminum-covered plate of food. "I think Eesa put a fork in there too."

Homeless Joe had never heard his angel referred to as Eesa before. *Assumedly a nickname.* He thought to himself as he cautiously unwrapped the aluminum from the paper plate. The plate was warm in his hands, so he just held it for a moment or two, and tried to recall his last hot meal. It had been ages since a plate of food had warmed his gnarled and swollen hands. Sitting next to his new friend and holding his hot food, Henry could hardly believe his good fortune. He moved his cane to the ground and handed his precious doll head to Jordan as he began to eat his first bit of food since Friday morning.

Jordan took the doll head with a tinge of disgust, but soon dismissed it, setting it on the concrete next to him. Rubbing his hands together, he finally decided it was safe to pull out the cigarettes that were burning a hole in his pocket. "Do you smoke?" He offered a cigarette to Isabel's friend.

Henry slowly shook his head.

Shrugging his shoulders, Jordan pulled one out and lit it up. "Really, I don't smoke either. I mean, I quit a year ago. It's just been one of those weeks, you know?" He explained as he took his first puff in over a year. The smoke filled his lungs like a warm blanket, touching a part in him that he felt only his Camel's could reach. He exhaled deeply, letting go all of the week's worries. "I don't know if Isabel told you, but her dad died a few days ago. Thursday night or Friday or something." He took another puff, closing his eyes as he let it all out. As he exhaled, he continued talking. "You should have seen her when RJ told her." He waved his cigarette in front of his face. "Stone." Shaking his head, he continued smoking. "It was like she didn't even care. Not upset, not happy. Nothing."

Henry watched the nervous man next to him quietly, trying not to let his sloppy chewing interrupt Jordan's venting. He appeared to be a nice man, so Homeless Joe kept listening to him as he ate the warm lasagna. As Jordan stopped talking to enjoy his cigarette, Henry thought back to his wife's lasagna. She had been a wonderful cook.

"We were a little nervous about how cold she acted. I mean, if my dad died, I'd want to know about it. I'd be pretty shaken, you know?" Jordan interrupted Henry's short daydream. "Then she goes to sleep Friday night and has these unbelievably graphic nightmares, or night terrors or whatever they're called." He shook his head and pulled out another cigarette. "So she's been sleeping in my room since then because I'm the only one who can stand her screaming." Lighting the next cigarette and smoking it down like the addict he was, Jordan shook his head. "So I've been sleeping on the floor and hearing her go through this for two nights now. I'm telling you, Joe," he itched the back of his head, scattering ashes onto the pavement, "I can't take it anymore. During the day, she's fine - except that she won't eat anything but jam. She eats it right out of the jar on a spoon, and she won't eat anything else. Then all night she'll have nightmares about her dad raping her."

Upon hearing this bit of news, Homeless Joe sat up a little straighter and turned his full focus on Jordan. He never knew that about his angel. In all of his visits with Isabel, she never mentioned her parents. Henry let the woman discuss whatever was on her heart. The topic just never happened to be her parents.

"RJ's handling it all pretty well, considering everything. He just can't deal with hearing her at night, which I'm beginning to understand." He blew out a mouthful of smoke. "I've got to tell you, Joe," he sucked on his cigarette, "I love her so much. Like, I really... love her, you know?" The honesty shocked him. It scared him how easily the words slipped out. He'd have to be more careful. He coughed. "I just don't know what to do. She says that she's fine with it, but she won't go to the viewing. She won't eat anything but jam. Jam!" He blew the smoke away from Homeless Joe. "That girl... I just... I mean, I do, Joe. It kills me to even think about her dad and that whole mess. I mean, I would be out of my mind if she even kissed me." Jordan laughed nervously and craved another cigarette, even though he had not quite finished the one between his fingers. "He just took her, you know? How can you..." His voice trailed off into no man's land, where his private thoughts about her usually ended up. Flicking the ash off of the tip, he took one last drag, holding the smoke in as long as he could. He wished that the smoke would fill him, either healing him or killing him. On the exhale, he realized that neither of the two solutions were feasible. "I would do anything for that girl, you know? I guess I just have to accept that there's nothing I can do. I don't know, Joe. If she just said the word, I would quit all this 'best friend' business. I really would, Joe." Jordan admitted to no one but the man who could not tell a soul. With frustrated angst, he put out his cigarette. The craving had been temporarily satisfied, so he put the remainder of the pack back in his pocket along with the lighter.

Realizing how much personal information he had revealed, Jordan understood why Isabel cared about Homeless Joe so much. In a strange and unexplainable way, Jordan was beginning to respect him too. Carefully studying the doll's head resting beside him, Jordan realized how little he actually knew about the man sitting next to him. Handing the doll's head back to Joe, Jordan patted him on the back. "I've got to get back before Eesa starts to worry. It was nice talking with you, Joe." Jordan nodded his head politely. He felt the urge to hug the man after sharing all of his secrets with him, but recalled his testosterone and refrained. He stood up, and then suddenly remembered the other secret that only he and Homeless Joe knew about. "Hey, Joe? Do you think we could keep the smoking thing just between us? Eesa and the guys wouldn't be too happy if they found out that I caved." Jordan stated his case, his guilt beginning to surface. "And could you not tell her I said all those things?"

Henry slowly nodded, noting that day as a special one. He had received a new friend, a hot meal, and trust. Those three things were not often in his possession, so he accepted them with his first ounce of dignity he had acquired in a long time.

"Thanks, man. See you around, Joe." Jordan walked back to the apartment a little lighter, and as he leaped past the doorman and up the stairs, he realized that he understood Isabel a little better. The feeling of being let into her secret world brought a relaxed smile to his face. Before returning to the busy apartment, he made a pit stop at his own place to brush his teeth and spray his clothes down with fabric deodorizing spray. The light and fuzzy sentiment left him temporarily when he remembered the cigarettes in his back pocket. Returning for the first time in a long time to his bad habit, Jordan felt guilty as he put his cigarettes and lighter in the very back corner of his closet, along with the rest of his demons. The secret hiding place was in the pocket of an old spring jacket stored in the furthest corner of his closet. Slumping his shoulders only slightly, Jordan returned to the party with the necessary two-liter of pop.

"What took you so long?" Isabel walked up to him, lightly bumping him with her hip. "Thanks for running out for me. Did you give Joe his food?" She asked, looking out at her family.

"Hey! Where'd you go?" Joey slapped Jordan on the back. "You missed it! Grandma sprayed Aunt Maria with the hose from the sink, and Aunt Nina's been going crazy with the whipped cream can. She's been spraying all the kids if they don't sing to her." Cousin Joey laughed and tried to shield Isabel and Jordan as Aunt Nina made her way to them. "Run, Jordan, run!" He warned, holding his hands out to stop her.

Never try to stop a strong-willed Italian woman.

"Don't you hide from me, my Jordan! I knew you would be coming back, and I have a special song for you to sing for us!" She beamed.

Not quite willing to argue with a woman so heavily armed, Jordan nodded and stepped out from behind Joey. "Okay, Nina. I'll only sing if you'll be my backup singer." He yanked on her elbow, clearing a small space for them to perform.

Thrilled that someone was playing along with her, Aunt Nina agreed to the proposition. "Okay, funny guy. Your song is 'I'm a Little Teapot', and really sell it!" She joked, smacking her hands together in anticipation. "This one's for the big money." She stood behind him, placing the whipped cream by her feet. Aunt Nina had six children, so her mind was perpetually stuck on nursery rhymes and silly songs.

"One, two, three!" She counted off. Away they sang at the top of their lungs. That was the only way to be heard over all of the hooting and hollering. Complete with all of the hand motions, the two adults sang the children's song, even remembering to bow at the end. The whole room applauded and cheered for them, and even reserved RJ had to smile at the scene.

"My wife! Isn't she beautiful?" Uncle Juliano broke through the mass of family members to kiss his wife, who was still bowing and blowing kisses to her adoring fans.

Isabel rescued Jordan before the hugging and kissing could repeat onto him. Pulling him to the back of the kitchen, she began laughing as he hugged her. "Your family gets weirder every time I see them." He was still grinning from ear to ear.

"The worst part is that you totally act like one of us. So now who's the weird one?" She walked over to the fridge and pulled out her strawberry jam.

Geoff intercepted her on the way to the silverware drawer. He slammed the drawer shut with his backside and did not budge for Isabel. "No way, Princess. Look at all of this wonderful food. You are not going to eat that nasty jam tonight." He laid down the law. Geoff was not very assertive, so Isabel did not know how to take his direct command. "Your family made you all of this great food, so you need to eat it."

Isabel huffed and tried to push him out of the way. "Give me a break, Geoff. Leave me alone." She tried to ignore his warnings.

Who knew why Groff grew a backbone that day. He was not the type to care about anything enough to stand up for it. He was easygoing and usually avoided confrontation like the plague. Often the people pleaser, Geoff rarely stood in Isabel's way. He had great respect for women, and being the youngest of five older sisters made him go out of his way to help the fairer sex more than hinder them. Clearly the strawberry jam was a moral issue for him. Geoff had this inherent do-gooder conscience that prohibited him from tolerating destructive tendencies in people. This targeted mostly women people - especially the women people whom he cared about. Even though Jordan was usually the one to harp on Isabel about taking care of herself, Geoff for some reason felt it was his responsibility to pull her aside this time.

"Don't you think I won't call Grandma over here right now and tell her that you have not eaten since Friday. Don't make me tell Tammy over there who barely eats because she thinks that she's fat that you've stopped eating altogether. If you're so hell-bent on self-destructing without even admitting that there is something wrong, then I'll bring Uncle Andy over here so that he can pray over your strawberry jam and call you every day of your natural life." Geoff started talking much louder.

Turning as red as the strawberry jam in her hand, Isabel took a step back from him. "Be quiet, Geoff." She looked around to make sure that her family had not heard Geoff. "Fine. I'll eat dinner. You know, I'm not opposed to eating. I've been eating." She lowered her voice so that only Geoff could hear her. "I just can't eat anything else. I don't know why, but I can't do it." Hanging her shoulders in shame, Isabel wanted to disappear completely. When Geoff touched her arm to hold her, she shriveled away from him. "You got your way. Now leave me alone." Because it was Geoff, she swallowed her pride along with six bites of gooey lasagna and one lonely meatball. Each ounce of food sat like a brick in her stomach, making her queasy. Anger towards Geoff stirred within her as he watched her barely eat. "Would you stop looking at me?" She snapped at him. Throwing her plate away, she spoke quietly with a scowl. "I hope you don't think I'm not mad at you." She turned to walk as far away from him as she could. Her pride had been wounded by Geoff speaking to her like the child she was. What made her the most furious was that Geoff had the audacity to tell her how she should handle the situation. Geoff had two parents who loved him. She had no parents and a brother who barely spoke to her, so jam every day did not seem like anorexia or like denial. It felt like her only path. She could not explain it to him, and felt stripped of her right to react in her own way.

"Don't think that I don't love you." Geoff echoed her words with his own sadness. "Sweetie - " He softened as she walked out into the mess of people. He had not wanted to upset her or control her. He was scared for her and wanted to help. Even after all of her adult experiences, there were parts of her that were still untouched. In a few ways, she was still innocent. The boys tried not to push, for none of them really understood the mess that was her adolescence. Most of the time they just left her alone to sort through the seemingly nonexistent emotions, though they made sure to step in with a hug whenever necessary. It was rare for them (especially Geoff) to step in and stop her.

Grandpa had captured Isabel and whisked her into the center of the party. Adela was still gazing up at RJ, who had not stopped nervously rambling. It was an all-time record for consecutively linked sentences that RJ had managed to lace together. The whole family took notice of the immediate change in his behavior, dubbing Adela as the miracle worker. Jordan was still in the kitchen trying to console his roommate, who eventually grew so perturbed by Isabel's behavior that he decided to leave the party. Geoff turned in at eight o'clock, which was unusual for the social butterfly.

Ever since Isabel had violently pushed him during that first night terror, he felt that he understood her a great deal more. He saw that she was not trying to frustrate everyone. It was strange to watch her show nothing but indifference towards the deceased member of her family. Having no idea herself what she was feeling, her sleeping habits changed as well as her eating habits. Geoff saw that her body was rebelling against her. The most frightening part about the whole ordeal was that Isabel did not seem to care, but rather welcomed the invasion. He took it upon himself to care for her body. He figured that it was the only thing to do, since she would let him nowhere near where the pain was really hiding. Still, he was reluctant to accept that their friendship had been reduced to this. He gave up his last reserved ounce of hope that their usually chummy camaraderie would ever blossom into something more.

Indulging himself with an extra hot shower, Geoff tried his best to wash away his concerns about the past few days. He did not want to spend his evening off obsessing about the strawberry jam or worrying about going to the dreaded viewing with RJ. Toweling off and putting on clean pajama pants, Geoff retreated to his bedroom. He always made sure to sleep with the door shut, in the chance that Jordan would get out of his bed naked. Geoff was slightly less than thrilled about seeing his roommate walking around in his birthday suit.

Back at the party (which was supposed to be the family coming to comfort the loved ones of the deceased), dear old Grandpa was entertaining the masses by telling of his old life in Italy. At least once at every family gathering he would tell the same story with the exact same details. He would talk of the way the air smelled, the crazy man with three goats, how he knew he would marry Grandma the moment he laid eyes on her, and all the other details that the family never grew tired of hearing.

Being the closeted sensitive man that he was, Jordan listened to all of Grandpa's stories on the kitchen stool with Isabel on his lap. She fit so perfectly in his arms that the world seemed to quiet itself and slow down for those few precious moments.

Jordan took several snapshots with his mental camera as Grandpa finished his stories. Grandma looked on her lover with sheer contentment. Few things could make a room of twenty-three people stop talking and sit still. Few things could make everyone smile and a couple of women dab at their eyes with delicate handkerchiefs and worn shirtsleeves. Even fewer people were worth listening to with such respect. The grandparents were the jewels of the family. Of all the family gossip and missing or shameful links, the grandparents never let anything hinder the love they had for their family. That was what made that particular family strong. It was also what made them all listen to Grandpa with such respect. The love he had for his bride had only increased during the fifty-five years of their marriage, and it kept them young as they continued to love their children, grandchildren, and great-grandchildren. Moved by her grandparents' inspiring marriage, Isabel met Jordan's eyes, and they communicated to each other feelings of deep love that they would not dare to speak, for fear of shattering a near perfect friendship. Jordan wanted to kiss her so badly that for a moment he almost saw himself doing it in his mind's eye. His heart pounded as Isabel broke the magnetic gaze by fiddling with the hem of her shirt.

A few moments before Grandpa concluded telling his beautiful stories, Isabel felt a disconcerting stirring in her stomach. Sitting up straighter did not seem to help, so she stood up and stretched out her torso. "I'll be right back." She informed Jordan, deciding not to tickle his knee.

He nodded in response as he watched her walk away to the bathroom.

From across the room, RJ invisibly took notice of his sister's change in location as he listened to Adela.

With every step she took, she felt the few meager bites of lasagna mixing with the acids in her stomach. Her sugarcoated stomach had only been fed strawberry jam, so the heavy food began to cause a violent reaction. As the acid almost audibly gurgled, she grew increasingly nauseous. By the time she reached the bathroom, she could already feel the roller coaster of vomit slithering up her throat. Scared and humiliated, she lifted the toilet seat cover and began to bow over the bowl. As her knees hit the floor, the realization of what was about to happen hit her all at once. The bittersweet release soon came as she choked out the meatball, the six bites of lasagna, and three jars of strawberry jam that had been sitting in her stomach. Over and over the vomit spewed out of her mouth and nose. It jerked itself out of her with such force that even the tears that had been packed tightly deep inside of her began falling out of her squeezed shut eyes.

The vomit came and came as the woman cried and cried. It came for several minutes until she was finally emptied of everything. Quite a picture she made, slumped over the toilet, face down to the muck. Whimpering softly, she lifted her shaking fingers up to the silver handle and pulled down. Within seconds the mess was gone, though Isabel felt far from better. Standing was such an effort that it almost made her nauseous all over again. As she gripped onto the shiny white sink to steady herself, she caught a glimpse of her reflection in the mirror. The girl who stared back at her was ghastly, yet strangely familiar. Pinching her cheeks and lightly slapping them, she tried desperately to get back to her normal self. Her usually rosy cheeks were pasty white, and even her auburn lips had been washed of all natural color. They had turned a sick shade of gray, bringing out the dark puffy bags under her eyes.

Trying desperately to keep from crying, she turned from the mirror and looked for a towel to clean the bathroom with. Turning again to the toilet, Isabel made sure that the seat was clean. She could hear her family joking around and having fun on the other side of the bathroom door, and for a moment she silently wished that she could be as happy as they were. As her stomach settled, a sneaking suspicion swept coldly over her, leaving her with the feeling that she would never again laugh as they did. No matter how much she tried to forget about her dad and remember her mom, it usually came to her reversed. With every passing month she would be reminded of her father, which erased the goodness of her mother's memories.

In her sadness, Isabel pulled back the clear plastic of the shower curtain and took out the bar of soap from the sidewall. The voices in the living room ceased and the world stopped turning momentarily as the girl sunk down to sit on the floor. She was hunched over while handling the bar of soap, carefully smelling the pungent aroma. It was Dove brand soap, which was the only kind that Isabel would use in the shower. Of all the things about her mother that were lost somewhere in her past, one thing that helped Isabel remember her was the bar of Dove soap, the same kind her mother always used. Inhaling deeply, Isabel relaxed her shoulders involuntarily. The womanly scent of soft perfume mixed with a powdery smell filled Isabel's world.

"Eesa-baby! Look at your hair! Come on, let me fix it."

Her mother's silky voice came back loud and clear, filling the room. She had long, thick, beautifully sweeping hair that Isabel had fortunately inherited. Clutching the soap and shutting her eyes, Isabel took in another lengthy sniff.

"Look at you! One day you will be such a beautiful dancer. Show me your pirouettes again, Bella."

Tears were oozing themselves out of her eyes and drooling down her now red nose and cheeks. Isabel began to shake as her mind reeled from trying to wrap itself around the buried memories of her long buried mother. The walls seemed to be closing in on her as the tiny bathroom swallowed her up like an enormous vibrating vacuum.

Though she could not stop the swirling and the shaking, Isabel covered her ears in an attempt to shut out the painful recollections that followed her mother's death.

Death. Her spine would always stiffen when people would say that word. They tossed it around as though it had the same affect as words like "decaf" or "shoelace". They talked about what they had no understanding of. They did not know how shatteringly terrible that word was, or they would not use it so casually. Isabel held her head tighter.

Death.

Here it was, happening all over again.

The air she sucked into her shuddering lungs was strangely not the powdery soft scent of the Dove soap, but of thick beige-orange makeup. Makeup covering her mother's decaying body. The thick plaster smell of death was all she could absorb, and all that her skittish mind could focus in on. Moldy, stale, and thick rouge were her realities now. Picturing the image of death on her father sickened her even more, causing her empty stomach to turn over once again.

"Leave me alone!" She whispered desperately, keeling over and banging her head repeatedly on the shiny, hard tile. The demons and voices swirled around in her throbbing head as she continued to bang it forcefully against the hard ceramic. All she could hear were her teenaged screams and her father's careless laughter as she banged her head as hard as she could one last time.

Silence.

For moments she did not move. For minutes, blessed minutes, she did not think. She just lay in a crumpled ball on the floor until her mind realized that she was with neither of her parents.

A loud knock on the bathroom door shattered her silence. Who dared disturb her at a time like this? For several seconds she made no effort to move or reply. All she wanted as she laid on the floor was to get back to that silent place.

A loud cackle rose above the living room commotion, ripping Isabel back to the present. Gradually she located the sparklingly white tiled floor, and pushing off of it with both hands, she brought herself to a reluctant seated position. Raising her trembling hands, she slowly stood, hunched over the sink once again. As she stared at the tired girl in the mirror, she noticed for the first time two little wrinkles standing out under her eyes like deep carvings etched into a smooth tabletop. A harsh, bloody red mark gawked at her from her forehead. She wondered how it had gotten there.

Again the knock came above the laughter. "Just a minute." The tiny voice that escaped from her mouth broke when she replied. Her exhausted brain finally kicked into gear, attempting to bring her fully back to her present life.

"Eesa, let me in. It's me." Her brother's low voice came from the other side of the door.

Before responding, Isabel opened the medicine cabinet and pulled out the bright green mint mouthwash. She swished the strong liquid around in her mouth as quickly as she could in hopes of erasing the putrid aftertaste of regurgitation still lingering in her mouth and throat. The mouthwash was so powerful that it caused her tear ducts to rip open once again, letting out a thin mist. Quickly she sprayed the handy air deodorizer all over the bathroom in hopes of masking her many indiscretions.

"Eesa, I'm not kidding. Let me in." He tried not to draw attention to her, so he kept his voice soft and inconspicuous. RJ was not the guy who would rush to comfort a friend, or hug a crying girl, but his sister was a different story. He was used to watching her fall apart. After having to be the only parent in the house, he had gained a sixth sense about his sister. Even with lovely Adela on his arm to distract him, he still made sure to keep tabs on Isabel's whereabouts. When he saw her make a beeline for the bathroom, a sinking suspicion sat in his gut that she was falling again. As much as Jordan loved her, and as much as Geoff cared, no one knew the mess like RJ did. He knew it was too good to be true when she appeared to be unaffected. Even the night terrors were just the start of what was sure to be an uphill battle. Once again, their father was hurting her, and once again, RJ had to stop it. With one more warning knock, he quickly opened the bathroom door and glided in, shutting the door tight behind him.

In her not so lady-like fashion, Isabel spat the mouthful of mouthwash into the sink. "What are you doing?" She growled at her brother, straightening her spine.

"Are you sick?" RJ ignored her glare as he pushed the lock in on the knob behind him. He slithered past her to put the lid down on the toilet seat.

"No! Get out of here, RJ. You would think that I could at least have some privacy in the bathroom." She dried her mouth off on the fuzzy white hand towel. As she turned to exit, RJ caught her arm.

"Sit." He ordered. Of all the people Isabel could ignore, her brother was not one of them. Immediately she sat down on the closed toilet seat lid. Now he towered over her as he shut out all of the bull she had been storing up to shove at him. No longer would he tolerate her thick-skinned responses. Running his rough hand over his tired face, RJ let out a deep sigh. "If you are not sick, then why are you throwing up?" He asked, getting right to the point.

Hardly anyone got to see this side of RJ. This was the closest he ever came to showing his feelings, and he made sure that the door was locked tight before doing so. Leaning his side against the cold sink, he crossed his arms over his chest like the father figure he was to her. His brown eyes narrowed, conveying hostility to the embarrassed girl below him. Buried not so deep past the anger was concern. He did not want his sister to be affected like this. No matter how hard he always tried to protect her, it was never enough. Clearing his throat, he spoke again. "I asked you a question."

All she felt was the anger. She knew that she was losing control over the situation. She understood for the first time the reality of the fall. What she failed to see was that her brother was on her team. She saw him as she always had, angry with their father and wanting to quietly fix her. Isabel did not want anyone to think that either of them had problems, so often times RJ's help was unappreciated.

RJ worked very hard to eliminate obvious external problems. He worked diligently for General Motors and paid more than his share of the rent. When their father went to jail, he was the one who got Isabel emancipated at the age of seventeen so that they could live together. He was the one who paid for most of her therapy, though he could never bring himself to go. When his sister could not afford college, RJ was the silent one who signed the check without question or harbored resentment. He wanted above everything else to see his sister shine. In the back of his mind RJ thought that if she could live a normal life, then he would also have a decent shot at one.

That had not quite happened yet, despite Isabel's many successes.

Staring uneasily at her squirming feet, Isabel shook her head. "I don't know, RJ. I think I ate too much."

RJ did not flinch. The brick wall stared at her with such intensity that she dared not look up. Twisting the skin on her knuckles nervously, she offered no further information.

There was a certain irony in the laughter that existed on the other side of the locked bathroom door. No one but Jordan had even realized that the hosts of this "party" were not even visible. Even Aunt Nina was preoccupied, busily interviewing the newest addition, Adela.

The very second that Isabel had left his lap, Jordan felt the creepy lingering haunt of his cravings coming back. Without willing them to do so, his sturdy hands touched all four of his pants pockets to check for the cigarettes that were clear across the hall and stashed away in his closet. His lips pursed involuntarily as he ran his tongue slowly in between his teeth and his upper lip, anticipating the taste. Before his conscience could even kick in, Jordan was off his stool in hot pursuit of his saving grace, those cursed cigarettes.

Past the family, out the door, and into the hall he flew, pausing only to smile at their neighbor who was just getting in.

Tom worked the afternoon shift at the steel plant on the east side of town. Of all the people living in the six-story apartment building, Tom was the only person that Jordan would chat with besides the doorman. People tended to keep to themselves mostly, breaking the silence with a quick forced smile every now and then. Tom did not have a family, many friends, or a girlfriend, so his occasional conversations with Geoff and Jordan helped to temporarily fill his lonely void.

Just then, Jordan did not have conversations with Tom as a priority. His tunnel vision had narrowed in on the contents of the jacket pocket stashed away in the back of his closet.

Traveling faster than he had in quite some time, Jordan flew straight through the apartment and into his room. Within seconds he was lighting up his cigarette and opening up the bedroom window. With shaking fingers, Jordan struggled to keep from dropping his contraband onto the street below. As he inhaled, the emptiness that shook him off of the stool in Isabel's kitchen was temporarily filled. There was something unsettling in him that was growing increasingly uncontrollable. Whether it was the lack of sleep, Isabel's dad, or the kiss that he never had the courage to pursue that set him off, he did not know. Whatever caused the emptiness in him, cigarettes were the only feasible cure.

Back at the neighboring apartment, people were beginning to realize that it was nearly ten o'clock. Not wanting to leave without kissing the hosts, they soon began to realize that RJ and Isabel were nowhere to be found. Mary Katherine knocked on the bathroom door, hoping for Isabel.

"Isabel? Are you in there?" She asked in her most polite voice. Mary Katherine was Aunt Nina's oldest daughter.

Isabel was still huddled on the closed toilet seat, and did not know if she should answer or not. The second she opened her mouth to call to Mary Katherine, RJ held his hand up to silence his sister. "No, it's RJ." He answered. Once again, he would handle this.

"Hey, RJ? We're going to take off soon." She tapped her nails on the door.

"Okay. I'll be out in just a minute." He called to the locked door, still not breaking his stony stare at Isabel. He would fix this. Somehow he would fix this.

Lowering his voice to a steady, deep tone, he prodded a little bit more. “I don’t think you’re eating, Bel.” RJ was firm in his assumptions. "How are we going to fix that?"

Anger flared up in her eyes and turned her blood hot. "I hate that you are always trying to fix me. All three of you." She blamed RJ for the seeming sin. "I am not broken! I hate that you all take shifts trying to put me back together, when nothing is wrong!" She declared defiantly.

RJ's eyes bulged as he rubbed his hands down the sides of his face. "I don't think there's a word to describe the amount of denial you push at us. You know why we have to come in here and pull you out of your own puke? You know why we have to force you to eat actual food? You know why we have to wake you up from screaming about Dad? You know why we have to fix you? It's because *you* aren't fixing you." RJ's stomach started to feel like something was burning a hole through it. "Gosh, Bel, you call this normal?" He pointed to the obviously bloody spot on her forehead. "How did you even do this to yourself?"

She touched her forehead curiously and was surprised to see a small mark of blood on her finger. Shifting on the cold seat, she swallowed, moving from angry to embarrassed. "I swear, RJ. If you're trying to make me cry, it won't work. I can't think about Dad. I won't." She refused to say another word about her father, given that she was dangerously close to feeling things that only her subconscious was willing to touch.

His emotionless and controlled demeanor changed as soon as the words escaped her mouth, and he saw her chin begin to tremble. With his arms still crossed, he leaned forward ever so slightly and shifted his weight to the other foot. His mouth ran about four seconds slower than his brain at all times, so pursuing a conversation with RJ took a great deal longer than with anyone else. "I'll get you help." He reached for any possible solution. Seeing his sister hold her head up stubbornly as she refused to cry struck a chord of compassion in him. He knew that even though he had her cornered, she still would not admit that she had a problem that was gradually becoming too big for her. Feeling as though he had hit the wall and could not press her anymore, he sighed as his shoulders deflated. "Are you going to the viewing?"

Not even acknowledging the issue, a different question spewed out of Isabel's mouth. "Are you sad that he's dead?" Nothing else would stick in her mind except for that one haunting question - which was the root of her present dysfunctions.

RJ would not even attempt to answer his sister. Instead he slowly brought his hand to her shoulder and held it uncomfortably, trying to conjure up an answer to the question that he had not even poked at yet. "Bel, it's okay if you are. It's okay if you're not. Just at least be honest with yourself." Realizing that he had been speaking way more than his normal comfort level would allow, he swallowed, put his hands in his pockets, and crooked his head to the side. "I've got to go say goodbye to everyone, so why don't you stay in here? I'll send Jordan in here in a few minutes to talk to you, okay?"

When her brother exited the narrow bathroom, her dark emotions were already beginning to evaporate. Using the mirror as her guide, Isabel mopped up some of the blood on her forehead with a few tissues until it did not look quite so heinous. With much effort, she proceeded to brush her teeth in hopes of getting that last flavor of her former breakdown out of her mouth. The circular motion of her toothbrush lulled her into a more relaxed frame of mind where she was free to breathe a little easier. Seeing her brother exude so much tenderness in a single day was a bit unnerving, but proved to be the temporary bandage she needed to open the door and face her family.

As she entered back into the noisy living room, her dark eyes surveyed the people, looking for her partner in crime. In the midst of her search, a large man caught her in a bear hug. "Goodbye, Isabella. We will see you tomorrow, right?" Uncle John smiled as he ruffled her pulled-back hair. Being a loud man, he never really did things halfway. If there was ever a taboo question that needed addressing, you could leave it to Uncle John to bring it to the surface.

No one turned to look directly at them, but the family quieted down considerably to eavesdrop. "RJ and Geoff will be there, but I can't go. I have work." She lied. "We'll see you at Thanksgiving in a few weeks though, okay?" Isabel answered, though her throat had gone dry.

A few people still pretended they did not hear her, but at that point most of the family had turned to stare at her. The quiet calm was unsettling, and being the center of attention made Isabel painfully shy. Also being witness to this public conversation was her brother who, once again, had to take action when his sister froze. "Hey, Eesa? Could you go find Jordan for me?" He made his way over to his frightened sister. "I know he'll want to say goodbye to everyone."

Isabel finally swallowed the knot in her throat and quickly exited to the haven across the hall. In a few short steps she was outside of her best friend's bedroom door - not to bring him back, but to be held until all the mishaps had disappeared. "Jordan, are you busy?" She rapped her knuckles on his purposefully shut door.

The four cigarettes he had left in the carton tumbled to the street far below him. Cursing, he contemplated jumping onto the street that lay stories below him to retrieve those last four cigarettes, but then decided that was against his better judgment. Quickly putting out his current cigarette on the outside wall of the building, he flung the smoking stick out the window. Used to having to hide his dirty habit, he had gotten quite good over the years at covering his steps. "Actually, could you give me a minute? I've got to change my shirt." He stood.

"Oh, sure." She stepped back, thinking it unusual that he would ask her to leave just so he could change his shirt. Jordan had always been a natural element kind of guy who had often been spotted walking around in nothing but his boxer shorts, and on more than one occasion, without the boxers. From the other side of the door he spoke. "Why don't you go apologize to Geoff while you're waiting?"

The misguided suggestion was convincing enough for Isabel's guilty conscience, so reluctantly she moseyed over to Geoff's closed door. Not really wanting to recall his scolding her, the thought of apologizing to her friend seemed to be the quickest way to right this miniature fight.

A light tap on the door was all it took to pull Geoff out of bed. On his way to opening the door in his befuddled daze, he tripped over his shoes that he had neglected to put away. Biting his lip to keep from cursing aloud, Geoff opened the door. "You okay?" It was all he could mutter as she entered his bedroom. The big toe on his left foot was throbbing.

"I'm sorry I snapped at you, Geoff." Though her arms were crossed, both shoulders slumped forward in sadness. Sometimes when she became nervous, Isabel would pinch herself until she said her piece. Clenching the skin covering her ribcage satisfied her whim in that particularly uncomfortable moment, and she continued. "It's sort of strange in my head right now. You're right; I should've listened to you. I don't know why I got so mad." She leaned back against the cold wall.

Turning on the bedside lamp, Geoff nodded his head. He sat back on his bed and stared up at his friend. There was something sad about watching her squirm that erased any grudges or negative thoughts he had been harboring about her bad behavior. Holding up his hand to her, he offered her a seat next to him on the bed. "It's okay, Bel. Things are stressful now, but I have no doubt that you will get through this just fine." He rubbed her back. "You'll be just fine." He concluded as she closed her eyes, leaning her heavy head on his shoulder. "Eesa?" He tried to call her out of the sorrow she was visibly feeling. "You've got a scrape. Man! What did you do?" He grasped her head in his hands and eyed her forehead. "You need to put something on that, Bel. Do you want me to fix it?" He touched her face gingerly.

Snapping her eyes open, she pulled away from him. "No, I don't want you to fix it." She sighed with her whole body. It deeply wounded Geoff to see her pull away from him so forcefully. "I'm fine." It was the only thing she could grasp at to say. Not really believing her own words put her in an even more desolate disposition. The room grew quiet as they both pondered things that they were unwilling to say. Not knowing which emotion to pick, Isabel temporarily denied them all.

"Bel, I'm real tired." Geoff rubbed his face and yawned. Too many shifts at the hospital were beginning to take a toll on him, and at that point, he knew that if he did not rest soon, he would say something to her that he would regret. They both stood and embraced in a long, exhausted hug, silently forgiving each other. "You'll be fine, Bel. I'll come and wake you up tomorrow before I go, okay?" Geoff paused to kiss her hair that still smelled faintly of flowers and coconut. "If you want to lay down with me and take a nap, you're more than welcome to." He silently prayed that Bel would choose to stay with him that night.

Pulling back the covers, Geoff flopped back onto the warm spot on his bed. Isabel tucked the covers up around her friend's neck as he closed his eyes to keep from watching her leave. "Rain check." She shook her head. "I've got to go clean up the apartment. Goodness knows what'll happen if I leave it all for RJ to do, right? The food will be left out till next week if I don't get over there." She smiled down at him. He looked so precious to her, all buried in his covers. "I'll see you in the morning, Geoff." Turning off the lamp, she exited the room.

Geoff received the sleep he needed so badly, and he proceeded to spend the night snoring rather loudly in his bed.

Assuming that Geoff was asleep, Isabel laid on the couch as she waited for Jordan, who was currently in the bathroom brushing his teeth. Time passed slowly as she hugged her stomach on the couch.

Back at the other apartment, RJ was successfully herding the crowd out the door. Being hugged and kissed (and even pinched on the bottom by Aunt Maria) took a lot out of him. Always the master of finesse, RJ stood at the door shooing each member of his family out into the hallway, grunting a quiet "thanks" to them as they left. One by one they left, then two by two, then whole households, until only Grandma, Grandpa, Gina, and Adela were left. Grandma made a list of things for Adela and Gina to help her with in the kitchen. They were trying to find places for all of the leftover food so that the two men could have some time to talk.

"You are a good man, RJ." Grandpa slapped his grandson on the back as the men sat down on the couch. Grandpa shook his head and smiled. "You take such good care of my granddaughter. You will make an excellent father someday." The twinkle in his eye sparkled brighter than usual. He loved RJ and thought of him as his own son, and RJ in return saw his grandfather as the perfect father he had lost long before Friday. "In fact, I saw you with that young lady tonight. Gina's friend, Adela. What do you say about her?" The cause for the sparkle became evident to RJ.

"Grandpa, I just met her. She doesn't even know me." He glanced over at her, his eye catching on her golden hair. "What makes you think that she would even want me? I don't know if you've noticed, but I'm not exactly the dating type. I happen to be the working type." RJ could not look away from her. She looked so perfect and beautiful even while completing the simple act of stacking up the dishes. There was something about a domestic woman that turned him on. That was why he was so attracted to Geoff's sisters. They were all homemakers, with the exception of Gracie who worked at the bank three days a week. Adela's blonde curls were pushed back behind her ears, revealing her pale peach complexion. RJ shook his head slowly, captivated by the new doe. "She definitely wouldn't want me." He concluded.

"Just take her for a walk, RJ. The more you talk to her, the more you will fall for her. Give her a chance to know you." Grandpa patted his grandson on the back. "Put your life on hold for one night, son. Let Jordan and Geoff stay with Isabella. She will be just fine."

RJ's spine tingled with the warmth that came when his grandfather called him son. His stomach compensated by churning, and then his mind immediately shifted to the rapidly approaching events.

"Grandpa, I know there is no funeral or anything, but who do I need to see about the casket and the headstone?" Talking about financial matters was much easier for RJ to process than his own emotions.

Grandpa sat back and pulled an envelope out of his pocket. "Your father's life insurance covered the casket and a small headstone." The grandfather looked at his feet as if he had been trying to find words appropriate for this moment. Making sure not to look directly at his grandson, the man reached into his own worn pocket and pulled out a crinkled white envelope. Extending the envelope to RJ, he swallowed. "This is what he left for you kids." He exhaled as the envelope left his hand and sunk into RJ's. "I was waiting for the right time to give it to you. He must have been doing well after he got out of prison. This is what his family gets."

RJ just stared at the white folds in the envelope and let his mind go out of focus for a moment. It had been years since his father had given him anything. True, this was not exactly a gift, and it was not just for him either, but he hoped the envelope resting in his fingertips was enough to cover over some of the wounds a father leaves on his son. It did not matter what was in the envelope, he decided. RJ was content in having anything good that his dad would give him.

Standing up to bring his mind back, RJ patted his grandfather's knee. "Thanks, Grandpa. I'll see you tomorrow." The chatting women had just finished the dishes when RJ tucked the envelope into his pocket and walked over to the kitchen. Adela was sorting out the clean silverware and putting the forks into the drawer as RJ stood beside her. "Do you want to go for a walk, Adela?" He whispered softly next to her.

Blushing as the last fork slid into place, she glanced over at Gina, who was adamantly nodding. "Sure. You can walk me home. I only live about seven or eight blocks east of here." She wiped her wet hands off on the gray towel that hung on the oven and closed the silverware drawer carefully.

Thinking it would be much more difficult than that, RJ had not yet thought through his next move. "Okay. Let me get your coat." Quick came the protocol date behavior, and RJ did not stop himself to think of where this knowledge came from.

"We are leaving now, grandson. We will see you tomorrow." Grandma pinched RJ's cheek with her stiff arthritic grip. "Oh! I just love my little grandbaby! You are such a man, but you are still my grandbaby!" She shook her fat, crooked finger in his face.

"I'll see you tomorrow, Grandma." RJ stretched out his mouth as he passionately rubbed his cheeks, which now had red pinch marks on them. "Bye, Grandpa."

Grandpa shook his grandson's large hand and winked at Adela. "Goodnight, dear." Adela hugged Gina and said goodnight. As the last of the family members finally exited, RJ found himself exhaling at the thought of being alone for a while with Adela.

Entering Isabel's room, he found the only coat left lying on the bed. Almost as pure as its owner, Adela's perfectly white wool coat and cheery yellow purse were well suited for her obvious pastel fetish.

The chivalrous style in which RJ helped her with her coat came from years of watching Jordan and Geoff baby his little sister. He had not asked a woman out since he and Isabel had moved out together. The very few females who had been fearless enough to ask him for a date were the only semi-romantic evenings he had survived in those many years.

"Thank you. You know, I didn't get to really talk with your sister or your friends. They just disappeared. Do you think she liked me?" Adela inquired, looking up at RJ with her big eyes.

RJ just grinned as he handed her the dangling purse, feeling odd holding it. "She thought you were great and would have asked you out for lunch or something to play twenty questions, but she went to Jordan and Geoff's because she wasn't feeling well. I just need to stop in and check on her, and then we can go." He stepped forward and opened the door for her, calculating that as the next step on the dating checklist.

Immediately frowning, she smoothed back the hair that fell into her face. "Are you sure she'll want us to come over if she's not feeling well? I know that when I'm sick, I usually don't want to stay up and make conversation with strangers. Especially strangers who would flirt with my handsome older brother at his father's wake!" Adela boldly complimented him, appalled at her forward behavior. She covered her face in her hands and shook her head. He smiled and finally looked directly at her, being reminded of how much he was attracted to her.

Nervously scratching at the back of his neck, RJ shrugged his broad shoulders. “Handsome?” He savored the compliment under his breath. “Come on. Let’s go say ‘bye’ to everyone.” He tried to make it sound like a command, the way that he was used to ordering his sister around, but somehow the words came out as more of a suggestion rather than a stern order. He was starting to notice a change in his manner, and was not quite sure if he was equipped to do that gracefully.

Audaciously placing his hand on the small of her back, he led her out the door. RJ was surprised at how forward he was being, so he immediately removed his hand from her. The urge to both talk to her and listen to her flooded his brain, and surprisingly he chose so speak. “Eesa’s not really sick. All this funeral talk has been really hard for her, so I sent her to the guys’ apartment so she wouldn’t be as overwhelmed. My family means well, but,” RJ shook his head as he closed the door behind him, “I know she’d just as soon forget him than spend time honoring the family by going to the viewing.” Taking three steps forward landed them at their destination.

As he raised his hand to twist the door handle, Adela rested her hand on his arm to stop him. Still dazed by her constant electricity, his world stopped rotating for her. “Not to pry, but why wouldn’t she go to the viewing? Did they not get along?” Adela’s ignorance made her even more irresistible to RJ, who was still working on piecing together simple sentences. For a brief half of a second, he contemplated giving in to his id by grabbing her face and kissing her. Instead, he put his hand to his forehead to check for sweat.

“How about I explain it to you on the way to your house? Just don’t mention my dad or the viewing to Isabel, okay?" He opened the door to find his sister holding her stomach, curled face down on the couch. Inwardly he panicked, not wanting to reveal to Adela all of the skeletons they had worked so hard to bury. "Eesa, Adela wanted to come by and say 'goodnight'. I'm going to walk her home." He spoke, the words waking his sister from her thoughts.

Isabel sat up, a smile growing at the sight of Adela. Standing up, she walked to the other woman. "That is so sweet of you. I'm sorry we didn't get to talk more." She offered. "Please tell me that RJ's asked you out so I can at least have another chance to get to know you." She begged sincerely.

Adela looked at her shoes timidly. "Not just yet, but I'm hopeful." Her eyes crept from her shoes to his.

Isabel folded her arms and leaned back in her stance. "Well it was a pleasure meeting you, Adela. I know you just ate, or I would offer you something." She walked over to the bathroom and tapped the door with her knuckles. "Jordan, RJ and Adela stopped over to say goodnight before they go out for the evening." Adela had no idea how rare an occurrence it was for RJ to walk a girl home. After eight minutes of erasing the damage done to his breath and clothes by the smoke, Jordan needed only that simple sentence to get him out the door.

Opening the bathroom door, he smiled a clean, toothy grin at the newlyweds. In a few short steps he was shaking Adela's hand politely and thanking her in his most generous fashion for coming to visit with the family. He secretly hoped that no one could smell his cigarette smoke, or the excessive mouthwash and mints he had used.

The adolescent adults made their exit, and Jordan slapped RJ's hindquarters as he shut the door behind them. Isabel and Jordan held a silent dance celebration in RJ's honor, wiggling their hips with the enthusiasm of any true junior higher.

Coming down from the high brought about a sudden urgency in Isabel. It felt unnatural to her that RJ was adjusting and trying new things while she still felt trapped. Among the many things she decided that she needed in her life, one of them was to not turn into her brother, who always seemed angry and haunted. After her bout with the shiny porcelain toilet, it felt as though their roles had shifted. Now she was the angry one. As far as she knew, RJ's ulcer was not flaring up again. She was the one with all of the repressed turmoil. She was the one who could not sleep like a normal person. She was the one falling apart, she realized. Not knowing what to do with this new thought, a crazy idea crept into her brain. "Jordan, do you have gas in your car?" She asked, looking far away at nothing in particular. It appeared as though she was looking right through the wall and into the next apartment.

Spinning around to the beat going on in his head, Jordan nodded. "Yeah. Three quarters of a tank, I think." He said, swiveling his hips in concave half-circles.

"I want some fries. Feel like eating?" She asked, already unbuckling the imaginary cement shoes that had kept her from moving since they had left their old life so long ago. She didn't know why, but it was time to go back.

Surprised at her sudden suggestion and unexpected willingness to eat, Jordan stopped gyrating, and stared at her with a raised eyebrow. "Okay. Do you want me to run to McDonald's for you?" Although fries were a long way off from actual food, he was more than happy to fill her with grease rather than the same sugary jam she had stayed faithful to for days.

She shook her head and started walking to the kitchen. "Grab your keys." Pulling a pen out of the junk drawer, she jotted a note on a napkin for Geoff, telling him that they were going out for the night. Quickly she wrote a second note for RJ, and briefly exited to place it on her counter where he would see it. Returning to a slightly suspicious Jordan, she winked at him and pulled on his arm.

"Come on. Do you have the keys? Let's get out of here." Any comments Jordan wished to make to her were squelched as she turned her back to him and bolted into the hallway. Without even looking behind her, Isabel flew down the staircase, assuming Jordan would catch up.

There is no predicting her. Jordan thought to himself as he took his keys out of his black leather jacket and trotted after her. The other doors were all shut and locked tight for the night with little commotion seeping through to the hallways. For a moment Jordan entertained the thought of him and Bel having an apartment together. Pushing through the front entrance quickly reminded him to snap out of it. There she was, already waiting for him at the car door.

"Hey, can I drive?" She batted her eyelashes with high hopes of dramatically persuading him. Jordan was more than a little overprotective of his car, and for once could not be won over by her feminine wiles.

Moving her aside using only his left arm, he narrowed his eyes. "Where's your driver's license?" He unlocked the driver's side and opened it for himself. Isabel frowned as she realized her spontaneity had left her ill prepared. Jordan sat in the driver's seat and mimicked her frown. "Awe, too bad. You know, I don't understand why we don't take Old Faithful down to McDonald's. I think your car could push it that far." He teased quickly and shut the door before she could refute.

"I hate it when you call her that. Bessie runs just fine, thank you." She started arguing with him through the window.

With the window already rolled up and the door shut and now locked, Jordan turned the keys to the silver four-door and pretended to not be able to hear his friend.

"Jordan, would you stop it!" She smiled as she raised her voice. Walking around to find the passenger door locked, she pushed her petite fist to the windshield. "Open the door!" She cried in vain as Jordan turned the radio on to drown her out. He danced and bopped in his seat as she pounded and ranted on the outside. Growing weary of his shenanigans, Isabel just crossed her arms and stared at her dancing friend, refusing to be entertained. As the music beat picked up, Jordan grew increasingly more animated, eventually lifting his hips up to shake his butt at Isabel's window. This brought them both to giggles as Jordan finally unlocked her door. She sat in her seat with her eyes covered. "Ah! I'm blind!" She playfully smacked his shoulder with her free hand. "How am I supposed to claim you in public now?" She laughed.

"Public? The only people you hang out with are Geoff and I, and I'm pretty sure that Geoff would have been in the car pressing ham to you too." He backed out the car gingerly, as though he had a sleeping baby resting in the back seat without a seatbelt on.

"I have friends that aren't you two clowns." She raised her nose indignantly. "Oh hey, could you stop by Bessie for a second? I have to get something." She leaned forward in her seat.

"Yes, Miss Daisy." He obeyed, pulling up behind the deathtrap that was so fondly referred to by its owner as Bessie the Buick.

Isabel hopped out and grabbed her small black wallet out of her car, quickly sliding back in beside Jordan. As he pulled out of the parking lot, he let out a long, low whistle, looking at her sideways. "You are in so much trouble when I tell RJ that you still don't lock you car."

"I'm so scared." She buckled her seatbelt across her chest. "Get onto the freeway and head west." She pointed left.

Jordan shook his head disapprovingly. "And you keep your wallet with your license, credit card, and cash under the seat? Bel, now that's prime material for RJ hysteria. I can just picture the lecture now." He smiled as he turned left towards the freeway.

"Yeah, I bet he would freak out even more if he knew that I keep my spare key right next to where I hide my wallet." She stared out the windshield to help further navigate. "Get onto 75 south." She pointed.

Jordan laughed at her carelessness. "In all fairness though, I think Bessie's partially hanging off bumper and rust-infested body will keep away even the most desperate looters and car thieves. Besides, when they speed away in the car chase, they won't get very far seeing as how your car stalls whenever you hit, like, fifty." He ducked as she hit his arm. "And who knows? Maybe it'll be raining that day. Bessie stalls whenever showers are even mentioned in the forecast." He laughed at his own good humor. "I don't understand you. RJ and I both get great deals on GM cars. Why don't you just buy a new one?"

"Benedict Arnold." She hissed with a smirk. "Bessie has been faithfully toting me around for years. She was my mom's. You really expect me to just trade her in like she's a..."

"Car?" Jordan pulled the last word out of her mouth. Coaxing the gas a little, he sped past a slower driver and merged into the left lane. "She is a car. And I don't think you would get much for trading her in. Maybe the junkyard will take her for free. Though, you'd probably get more back as a tax write-off than from trading her in." Jordan set in on the advice-giving sermon. RJ was not very effective at communicating helpful lessons to his sister, so Jordan took over that particular facet of unnecessarily parenting Isabel.

Although she respected Jordan and usually listened faithfully, Isabel was too distracted to listen. The thought of reaching their destination was so clear in her mind that she found it difficult to absorb much else. Years had passed since she had been back to the old neighborhood she had grown up in. Every Friday night her parents would take her and RJ to Grille24 to eat. That became their family time in the early years before her mom died. After a weekend of strawberry jam, the only solid food she would stomach was a basketful of Grille24 spicy Cajun fries. The sweet jam binge had left her craving salt (along with some much needed sanity). There was not a whole lot of thought or reason that went into her sudden urge to return to her childhood, but whatever the root desire was, all she knew was that she needed a mouthful of those Cajun fries and a friend to share them with.

"Not that I mind doing your taxes, because I don't. I just think that it's something that we could do together." Jordan continued his advice. Isabel began nodding when she realized that he was still talking.

"Okay, 75 branches off. Follow it to the left." She instructed, raising her chin. "We'll be on that for a while." Her lower back snuggled itself into the cold leather seat.

A look of confusion and sudden revelation swept over Jordan's face. "Wait! Why are we on the freeway? McDonald's is right by Barney's."

"You just now realized that you were driving on the freeway?" She raised an eyebrow at him. Shaking her head slowly, she scolded him. "And to think I let you do my taxes." She smiled.

"First of all, you don't let me, you beg me. I don't sit around thanking my lucky stars that I get to do your taxes." He slowed his speed a little and let a faster car pass him by. "Second of all, where are we going?" Her unexpected adventurous spirit had caught him so off guard that he forgot to inquire as to where it was that they were going to.

Adjusting her rings with a smile, Isabel gave Jordan her most innocent face. "I already told you. We're getting fries." When Jordan did not look amused at her secretive antics, she gave in. "Okay, so the restaurant's not around here. You've got to trust me. These fries are worth the drive." She still had on a spotlessly naïve expression to entice him to forgive her misleading whims.

"Oh, fine." Jordan gripped the wheel and sighed heavily. "I'll take you anywhere you want, just quit looking at me like that. It makes me feel guilty, even though I know I couldn't possibly have done anything wrong. I mean, you're the one who tricked me into this in the first place. I should have known when you asked me if my car had gas." He leered, putting his whole right hand over her face to try covering it up. Sometimes he saw her as too adorable to turn down.

"Oh, you love it." She smiled as she fiddled with the radio stations.

Nearly two hours of banter had passed between them, and the only other two people with as much unspoken sexual subtext were RJ and Adela, who were sitting and enjoying scintillating conversation on the bench outside of Adela's apartment. Even though the evening was satisfactory, Adela did not invite him into her building as they said goodnight. They had spent close to two hours talking, but she began to notice that she was doing most of the sharing. While she felt a solid spark between them, a sneaking suspicion crept over her, convincing her doubts that she actually knew very little about the man walking her home.

Upon collecting his wits, RJ was the master at interviewing. He revealed very little about himself, while asking all about her. RJ found Adela fascinating. There was not a woman alive who looked as clean as she did. Perfectly pressed and curled, he was content in watching her and studying the little things about her as she talked. For instance, she sat perfectly straight with her soft chin always level to the ground. Each fingernail was delicately polished and filed to a length that RJ deemed as not too short and not too long.

"I know that I don't know you well enough to kiss you goodnight, but..." RJ walked with her the three stairs leading to her building, "...could I negotiate a handshake and possibly a phone number?" Knowing that he was being charming, RJ looked over at her and smiled.

Adela's eyes widened and her face flushed. "Um, I don't know, RJ." Her left foot moved a step away from him as they faced each other nervously.

Her half-hearted answer nearly shattered RJ's exposed heart, and the shatter showed up all over his face. Thinking he had completely offended her, RJ shook his head at himself. "I... I'm sorry Adela. It was nice to meet you." RJ suddenly realized how out of character he had acted all evening long. Talk to a beautiful woman? Walk her home? Ask for her phone number? This was definitely not anything he was familiar with.

"I want to see you again, but I don't know enough about you. I mean, you know more about me than most of my old boyfriends, and all I know about you is that you're not Catholic." She found her smile again.

"See, now I didn't know you had other boyfriends." RJ teased, regaining his recently exposed confidence. "I'm not trying to hide anything. I don't know, I guess I just like learning about you more." RJ was honest.

"I think that I would feel more comfortable giving you my phone number if I knew a little more about you." She pulled one of her curls behind her ear and cleared her throat. "Do you think we could try this again?" She offered. The pink of her dress gave her complexion a healthy glow, and as she was contemplating what to say next, she fiddled with one of the folds in the soft fabric. "You mentioned at your apartment that you're an engineer. Where do you work?"

RJ sighed as he mentally prepared himself to explain his life. "I work with Jordan at the General Motors office downtown. My job is to help oversee the new projects coming into the company. I look at blueprints for the newer models and work out the bugs." RJ looked to Adela's fidgeting hand and noticed that she was just as nervous as he was. A little relieved, he reached over and took her cold hand and rubbed it gently in both of his. "You are so cold." He observed, lacing her fingers around his. "What else do you need to know about me?"

Adela reddened and stood a little closer to him. She was love-struck by him and refused to stop smiling. "Tell me what your life is like. I met your sister and her friend. They seem nice. There was another friend too, but I don't remember his name. You work for GM. What else?" She blinked her beaming blonde eyelashes at him.

Shrugging, RJ laughed uncomfortably. "That is my life. That's my whole life. Those people that you met tonight are the only people in my life." Feeling that he was holding her hand too tight, he loosened his grip. "Other than my grandparent's house, or maybe the gym, work is pretty much the only place I go." He swallowed.

That was it. The secret was out. This mystery man was not the dream that every girl thinks all quiet and mysterious men are. At the end of the yellow brick road was not a wizard, but rather a lonely man behind the curtain hoping that people would not notice him, but look the other way instead. So he stood before the first girl he had had eyes for since high school, completely exposed and unnerved, waiting for a sign that all of the things that he was not would somehow be acceptable to her.

"You know," she leaned in closer to him and lowered her voice, "I've spent the last four Saturday nights listening to Frank Sinatra and putting together puzzles." She confessed with a secretive air. "At least you get to see your sister. My two older sisters live out of state."

"You're the lucky one. I am twenty-seven and I still live with my sister." He laughed at himself, rubbing her hand again.

"Speaking of your sister, why isn't she going to the viewing tomorrow? Was she not close to your father?" She prodded, stepping on toes with all of her dainty innocence.

Exhaling seemed to be the most appropriate response until he could gather his thoughts. "Do you want the long version or the short version?"

"Obviously the long version if you're letting me choose. You have an interesting family. I just love Gina." She hooked her hand through his arm and led him down the steps. "Let's go for a walk. I love walking when it's dark out. It makes me feel so dreamy. It's almost like we're the only voices in the city."

It did not take an explanation for RJ to comply with whatever the woman wanted. As they walked out onto the sidewalk, RJ began the twisted story of his family life. "Even the long version doesn't take much explaining. It's just my mom, dad, Eesa and me. Everything was normal, boring family life. Isabel was the baby, and I was the boss. She used to be sort of fat when she was little, so I nicknamed her Belly. Boy, she hated that." RJ realized that he missed his sister being chubby. He would gladly take that any day over watching her throw up jam. "Anyways, our mom died in a car accident when I was seventeen. It was a drunk driver - which is funny because she hated alcohol. She'd stop talking to my dad for days if he brought home a six-pack. She was so stubborn. But you know, she wasn't mean about anything. She was really gentle. She only yelled when we were really driving her crazy." Memories of his mother went much deeper than that, but RJ did not want to open that door all the way if he did not have to. "So my mom dies and that month Isabel drops like, twenty pounds. She was... fifteen? I think. My dad starts drinking. I'm thinking that he's just depressed, so he's exercising his freedom to drink now that mom's not there to stop him. A few months go by, Isabel getting skinnier and skinnier, and I start noticing bruises on her. They were like, on her arms and a few on her neck. I had lacrosse after school until late evening every night, so I couldn't keep an eye on her." The tension of talking about his sister wrapped itself around his stomach, grating on the thin lining and twisting his intestines like a dry sponge trying to wring out water. RJ stopped walking and rubbed his stomach. "Can we sit down somewhere? I guess I'm a little more tired than I thought." He tried to smile.

Adela nodded and pointed to a large, knotted oak tree. "Sure. How about right there under the tree?" She led him to the grass and helped him to sit down. Although the grass was cool and damp, Adela sat right next to him under the branches arching out from the tree, despite her thin, drafty dress. Being the good woman that she was, she lifted her hand to his forehead to check his temperature. Lightening the mood with her smile, she brushed her perfect fingernails through RJ's short hair.

The corners of RJ's mouth lifted as the sides of his cheeks dimpled. "Yeah, you could do that forever." He tried not to get carried away by her touch, but deeply craved more of it. Subtly he touched his shoulder to hers.

She took the invitation to cuddle happily, and felt much more comfortable now that he was being open with her. As she brushed through his spiky hair, she spoke softly. "Your sister had bruises?"

"Oh, yeah." RJ closed his eyes and enjoyed the female touch. "I thought it was her boyfriend. She was dating this jerk named Jake." He smiled. "I remembered his name because she scribbled it all over the front of her notebook." RJ sighed and gave her a sideways crooked smile. "Did you ever do that?" He asked.

A shallow wave of nostalgia painted her face. "Yeah. Tony Howell. I wrote his name everywhere. What grade was that? Hmm... wait a minute." She stopped herself. "You're doing it again. You're turning the conversation around." She accused him. "You were talking about Jake the jerk." Suddenly recalling her manners, Adela resituated herself. She folded her long legs together and pushed her heels to the side on the wet grass. Touching his arm reassuringly, she nodded for him to continue.

"Wow." He covered her hand with his. "You're tough. Umm..." He retraced the conversation. "Oh, so I thought it was Jake who was giving her the bruises. He only started liking her after she lost all the weight, and I just had a bad feeling about him." RJ's stomach muscles ground together as the conversation grew more serious. Talking about his current life was stressful enough, but adding the past to his plate was just a little more than he could handle.

To compensate for the angst, he let out a nervous laugh under his breath. "So my lacrosse practice is cancelled one day, and I go home early. Before I even set my bag and stick down, I hear my sister screaming this, this... terrified... So I run upstairs to her room, and there's my dad with his... and his pants down... and he's..." RJ was visibly in pain and holding his stomach as sweat ran down the sides of his face. Adela was shocked and beginning to worry about the man whose arm she was holding. "I just stood there and couldn't move. I don't know how long I watched him do... but then he started choking her and yelling at her to stop screaming so loud. I hit him in the back of the head with my lacrosse stick and punched my own dad until he was unconscious on the floor. My sister... just... and... for months she was scared and tried to hide it from me. She never told me any of it. My family... just... fell..." RJ trailed off and rocked himself back and forth to calm his nerves down. "He stalked her for a few months after he got out of prison. So I had a restraining order filed against my dad. It got so bad that I had to ask a few friends to follow her when I couldn't be there. I tried to be there, but I just couldn't watch her every second. Even now she checks in with me before leaving the apartment. I'm pretty sure she hates me for it."

RJ stopped talking to clear his throat and focus on breathing. "I don't want to talk about myself anymore." He breathed slowly as he gathered his thoughts. "Okay?" His stomach had taken just about enough stress. "I'm going to go home now. I have an ulcer, and my stomach is... I have to go home."

The night was beginning to fog over, giving Adela a slight chill. "RJ, I'm sorry I made you talk about all of that. I had no idea. Does Isabel need someone to take her out tomorrow? Like, to distract her or something?" Adela offered her services in an attempt to patch up the damage she felt responsible for causing. She shivered from the lower temperature that was rapidly filling the air. Her white coat was too nice to lie on the wet grass, so it was folded uselessly on her lap. "Wow, it's getting cold." Her obvious comment sent the chill to RJ as well.

"You are so... perfect." RJ shook his head and slapped the wet blades of browning grass off of his hands. "Jordan's taking her to do something tomorrow night. She's working too, so she'll be busy. Thanks though. You're so nice." He stood up, extending his hand to her.

"How about you? Do you need any help?" She took his strong hand and barely tugged as he effortlessly lifted her to her feet. The firm tug reminded her of the butterflies swarming around in her stomach.

A crooked half-smile took over his mouth as he teased her. "Well if you're offering, I could probably use a little supervision." He knew that Geoff would be proud. "Maybe this weekend?"

The insecure eyes did not match what came across as a cocky smile. Adela read his eyes and began to understand him a little more. Instead of dismissing the comment and saying goodnight, Adela ignored the warnings in her head and, against her predictable judgment, asked the question she had been itching to ask since they sat underneath the tree together. "RJ, would it be okay if I hugged you?" She dared to ask, using her very small, timid voice.

RJ's eyes grew wide and his palms began to sweat. "Um, yes. Yes, please." He nodded as he got over the shock of her normally impudent suggestion.

Without waiting for an awkward moment to overtake them, Adela all but flung her body into his arms. Tighter than she had squeezed anybody in a long time, she held him. As their hearts touched, a connection between the two almost strangers was firmly established, transcending attraction and puppy love.

The hug lasted nearly four minutes and ended with RJ slowly rubbing her back. "When can I see you again?" His husky whisper fell into her soft blonde curls.

Adela swallowed and forged forward in her attempt at bravery. "Would you take me to church next Sunday?" She cemented her forehead to his chest as she lowered her heels to the ground. "My pastor requires us to bring dates now. Darn liberals." She laughed at her own joke.

Without even waiting for his anger against the church to surface, RJ answered. "I'll take you anywhere you want, Adela."

Upon hearing her name on his lips, Adela lit up and gave him a quick squeeze. "Thank you." As RJ gave her one last embrace, she confessed. "That means a lot to me, RJ."

The wind picked up as they walked back to her apartment, hand-in-hand. After he walked her up the steps and they finally exchanged phone numbers, RJ walked the seven blocks back home floating on cloud nine.

For the first time in a painfully long time, RJ went to sleep with a smile on his face. Happy were his fantasies about taking Adela to church on Sunday.

Chapter Four

Far from sleeping and far from home, Jordan and Isabel were pulling into the half-full parking lot of Grille24. Perfectly content in knowing that he would give in to her whims at a moment's notice, Jordan shuffled ahead of her to open the fingerprint-stained door. Trotting past her friend, Isabel was ready for anything. Seeing the green and yellow tiling on the floor and the blue and yellow tiles climbing up half of the walls quickly pulled her memory back ten full years. Being mentally yanked back a decade is quite a feat if you have not lived much more than two.

Aside from a few new displays, the restaurant had not changed much. Even the golden spatula hanging directly above the small hallway towards the back was the same. On it was painted in green letters "Restrooms". The paint was slowly fading, starting with "R" and "E" being erased by the constant sunlight. The air smelled exactly as she remembered it, reeking of solid, greasy meat and heavy spices, with the inescapable stench of garlic haunting every dish that was served. With a grin from the hostess, she knew that she was temporarily fulfilled. This was her home sweet home. Now she would eat.

Jordan fought the urge to sit in the smoking section as he eyed a young beauty sipping her sanity from a long cigarette. It was all he could do not to walk over and kiss her just to suck the smoke from her pouting lips. Quickly turning to follow the hostess, he desperately grabbed onto Isabel's hand, hoping that her touch would cure him.

Isabel was preoccupied with her growing nostalgia, and did not squeeze his hand as he hoped she would. The hostess seated them in the specific booth that Isabel had requested. It was the exact same booth that she would sit in with her family every week and watch the cars drive past in the gargantuan picture window. When the hostess handed them their menus, Isabel held it up and giggled happily behind the food-spattered pages as she absorbed it all. Grille24 was her happy place. It was the land of two sane parents and a verbally non-stunted brother.

"Hi. How are you guys doing tonight?" The waiter greeted them without even looking at either of the two customers. Without waiting for them to answer, he cut right down to business. "What can I get you to drink?" He looked to be about Isabel's age. He had dark, permanently wild hair that made a point of hanging down near the eyebrow ring that rested above his left eye.

Jordan was still pouring over his menu, trying to decide his entire order. He did not like to wait to order his meals, and usually ordered everything when he chose his drink. "I'll take a Coke and a... a Mushroom Bacon Cheddar Burger... with fries." Jordan folded his menu up and thwapped it on the table to show that he was finished. He tried not to glance over at the vixen smoking in the corner.

"And your lovely girlfriend?" He turned his body toward Isabel, but still had not bothered to look up. His expression appeared to be bored. No, more than bored. His expression looked as though he could have been watching a rerun of Mama's Family for the sixth time.

Jordan shifted back in his seat at the unexpected observation. "Uh, what would you like, Bel? A big basket of those fries?" He picked up the dessert menu and fiddled with the flimsy pages.

She rolled her eyes at the waiter, and with a small smile she felt the need to tag on, "He's not my boyfriend." She took one more look at the menu before placing her order. "Well... Judas." She read his nametag. "Your name is Judas?" She questioned with very little tact.

He nodded and for the first time, looked at her. "My dad left my mom when she got pregnant. I'm her little reminder." Judas made a point of raising his eyebrows to end his life story.

"Wow." She soaked in the surprising information that made the two dimensional waiter all of a sudden grow an entirely new dimension. "I'm Isabel, and this is my best friend, Jordan." She felt the need to introduce herself to the stranger for bringing up a supposedly painful subject.

Judas' eyes stayed on her a moment before he spoke. "Isabel. Good to know. Can I take your order, Isabel?" He spoke her name as if she were an alien, or something to be oddly stared at instead of spoken to.

While Jordan rolled his eyes, Isabel ordered two plates of Cajun fries and water with lime as she tossed him her best almost-smile. The waiter moseyed off just as borderline comatose as he had been when he came to them.

"I can't believe you." Jordan shook his head at her.

Isabel shrugged and looked down at the dessert menu. "What?"

"What? You! Make the poor guy feel even worse about himself, why don't you. He can't help his name." Jordan whispered at her.

"Oh, please. I was just making conversation. The waiters used to be a lot nicer here anyway." She dismissed his comment. "Wait till you try these fries. They are amazing, and completely worth the trip."

Jordan scratched the back of his neck, growing anxious knowing that the long-legged woman over in the smoking section probably had an entire purse overflowing with cigarettes, and he had none. Running his tongue over his teeth, his self-control had worn thin and was about to snap. "I can't wait to try them. Did we pass a restroom on the way in?" He wiped his nearly sweaty hands off on his pants as he stood. Isabel nodded, noticing a slight change in his behavior. "Excellent." He craned his neck to see where the beautiful woman was sitting. Standing and towering over his friend, Jordan leaned down and planted an unexpected, mixed emotions kiss on her hair as he held the back of her neck. "The waiter was right, though; you are lovely." Taking a lengthy look at his best friend and hoping that it would heal him, he made his way to the bathroom.

Even as Judas brought the food to her favorite booth, Isabel was still mulling over Jordan's strange departure. His behavior took her by surprise so much that Isabel only barely acknowledged Judas' attempt at a smile. "So where's your friend, Isabel?" He made a point of saying her name. It almost sounded to Isabel like he was making fun of her.

Isabel shrugged. "He's in the restroom, don't worry." She eyed her fries, suddenly remembering why they had come all this way.

Still not looking at her, he sighed tiredly. "I was just beginning to." He set Jordan's food down at his place. "Alert me at once when he comes."

Her smile had faded completely, and was quickly being replaced by a glare that started at her eyes, and worked its way down to the corners of her mouth. "Are you having a bad day, or are you naturally this charming?" She inquired with the slightest bit of repressed hostility.

"What can I say? It comes with the name." He stood beside her table, now staring at her. She made it a point not to look up at him.

She could feel him looking at her, and it was beginning to ruin the perfect ambiance she had imagined her Grille24 experience to be. Tilting her head to the side, she raised one eyebrow in his direction. "Thanks, I'm all set here."

"Pleasure." He practically snorted as he left to attend to his other, no doubt satisfied, customer. Isabel was appalled at his behavior. Never had she received such attitude from a waiter before. Looking around, she wondered what was taking Jordan so long. Usually the lengthy trips to the restroom were taken after a meal eaten at Grille24. Her eyes surveyed the room, landing briefly on a tall man bent over, laughing with a woman in a tight red shirt. She recognized the man as Jordan when he turned his face up to the ceiling to laugh at the woman's obviously funny joke. Isabel shifted her weight towards the edge of her seat to stand up, but paused as she saw him take the cigarette from the woman's fingers and put it to his own lips. Isabel was temporarily stunned as she watched him smoke her cigarette, puff after puff. Still trying to keep up with her probably witty conversation, Jordan kept at least one eye open while he enjoyed the ecstasy of the borrowed cigarette. As Isabel noticed him looking up to locate her, she immediately buried her concentration in her plate of fries, pretending that they were incredibly fascinating. She did not dare look back up, for he obviously did not want to be seen by her. As she stared down at one individual fry, she began to think back over the small blips in his character over the past few days. Isabel was so intently staring at one of her long fries that she jumped when Jordan sat down across from her.

"Wow." He commented on her sudden scare. "You okay, kid?" Before she could nod or even acknowledge his voice, he spoke again. "Food's here already? That was fast." He quickly dove into conversation, as he did not want her to think he was acting strange at all. He had gotten his fix, and now he could eat. Surveying the supple greasy supper before him, he discovered the one essential supplement that was missing. "I forgot to ask for ketchup." He observed aloud, waving the waiter over. "You didn't order me ketchup?" He looked up at her, surprised, as though she had forgotten who he was.

Isabel was beginning to think that she was forgetting her friend as well when her thoughts were interrupted by the arrival of her favorite waiter. "Yeah, could I get some ketchup?" Jordan asked, not noticing Isabel's stare boring a hole right through him. The longer he sat across from her, as though nothing was at all different, as though he had not started up his old bad habit again, she changed from stunned to agitated. *Why would he do this to himself? Why would he hide it from me? What else could he be hiding? How do I act normal? Should I pretend that I don't know what he's doing to himself? I can't believe he would do this and not tell me!* She thought while averting her bewildered eyes. Without thinking, she picked up a fry and curled her arm to place it in her mouth, when she stopped and starred at the hot fry. This did not feel right.

"Oh!" Isabel suddenly remembered. "Could I have some mayonnaise too?"

Judas looked down at his order pad, and then scribbled something on one of the crinkled pages. Again, without looking up, he sighed. "Um, no." He answered, walking away with no further explanation.

Jordan just stared at the waiter as he disappeared. His surprise took on the form of a smile as he eyed Isabel. "I have to say it, that guy is hilarious." His eyes rested on his companion. "What did you say to him while I was gone?" He asked, sipping on his pop.

Isabel just shrugged her shoulders as though she could not think of a justifiable reason that their waiter would talk to them that way. "Sorry I forgot about your ketchup." She offered, still debating whether she should say something about his smoking or not.

Jordan dismissed the waiter's strange behavior as he poked at his burger. "Some wife you are." He teased. "You would think that you would remember that a burger is no burger without a separate pile of ketchup to dip your burger in."

Isabel decided to forgo the inevitable conversation about his smoking, and half-heartedly participated in his banter. "You just like being married without the responsibility." She poked at her fries, truly missing the mayonnaise.

"You know what I need, and we take care of each other." He picked up a large, curly fry. "And the sex!" He said a bit too loudly with a quick wink.

"Well the sex is why I joined in the first place." Isabel picked up on his sarcasm. "The sex, and the fact that you're going to let me drive your car on the way home."

"Funny. And it's not the army, Bel. Marrying me is the best decision you've ever made. I cook for you, I drive you across the state, I put up with your bad morning attitude (and breath), and I pick up the bill at cheap 24-hour greasy joints. I baby you mercilessly." He patted himself on the back.

Isabel sat up straight. "And what about me? Being your wife certainly has its drawbacks. I deal with you first thing in the morning *every* morning. I put up with your superiority complex."

"What!" Jordan guffawed as Isabel stood to sit next to him. Squeezing in and rubbing his stomach, she tried to discretely sniff his clothes to pick up any hint of smoke.

"Yes, superiority complex. All three of you walk around measuring your penises to my vagina." She eyed him, trying to will the confession out of him. "I stay faithful to you even though you're getting chubby."

"Chubby! I am not chubby." He tried to ignore the big, prodding eyes she was throwing at him.

"Oh yeah? Then what is this?" She pinched a wad of his stomach skin in between her finger and her thumb. "Good thing I signed that prenuptial agreement." She teased him wickedly as punishment for hiding his new smoking addiction from her.

Jordan's eyes were wide and his mouth opened and closed several times in disbelief before actual words came out. "I can't believe you just did that! You just called me fat!" He rubbed his side where she had pinched him.

Just to rub in her obnoxious point, she wrapped her arms around his neck and kissed his cheek, secretly trying still to smell how much smoke was on him. "That's okay. Most women like their men with a little extra padding."

"That's it! Get off of me! You think that I want you hugging me after you pinch my stomach and call me fat? I'm surprised that you even fit in the same booth with me, I just take up so much room." Jordan tried to wiggle away from her, causing them to both laugh out loud.

Isabel nuzzled his neck with a faltering smile as she noticed Judas coming with the coveted condiments. "Enjoy." Judas shot forth his monotone presentation.

Jordan rested his chin on Isabel's head and sized up the waiter. "Thanks, man. We thought you were serious when you said we couldn't have our stuff." He sneakily snatched up the ketchup before the waiter decided to take it away from him.

"I guess that's my charm." He eyed Isabel, who was growing curiously frustrated with their waiter. "Will there be anything else?" He asked, not taking his eyes off of her.

"Thanks; we're all set." She jutted her chin out to him and widened her eyes.

As he walked away, Jordan pulled his head away from Isabel's forehead to look at her directly. "Do you like that guy?" He looked down his nose at her suspiciously.

"Oh, shut up and eat your burger." She pulled one of the baskets of fries closer to her and took a long sniff, now expecting everything to smell of smoke. Remembering that this was her happy place, she decided to put the cigarettes out of her mind as best she could so that they could really enjoy Grille24. "Wait until you try this. This is the only way to eat these fries, trust me." Holding up a limp fry she had dipped in the thick mayonnaise, Isabel grinned, revealing her shiny, white teeth. "Open." She commanded.

Keeping his mouth wisely stapled shut, Jordan moved his head back to avoid the intrusive fry. “Eesa, that is sick. Not quite as nauseating as your jam mania, but it’s pretty close.” Usually he would not have a problem complying with her quirks, but as she was getting more difficult to predict, he was less willing to tag along with her strange idiosyncrasies.

“Oh, come on. RJ eats it like this too.” She waved the hideous fried cholesterol covered in fat in front of his frowning face.

Dipping his hamburger in a freshly poured pool of red goopy ketchup, Jordan protested. “No, he doesn’t. He eats them with ketchup. Like a man!” He recalled, taking a large, satisfying bite out of the overloaded burger.

“He eats Cajun fries with mayonnaise. I taught him how.” She emphasized her point by shoving the dripping fry into her mouth. “It's *so* good.” She licked her already greasy fingers.

With his mouth filled with burger, he tried to speak clearly. “You call me fat when you’re eating fries with mayo? You’re the one who’s going to be hitting the gym tomorrow.” He commented as he pinched the outer flesh of her thigh. “It’s about time you put some fat on all those bones.” He took another bite and grinned, showing off his mouthful of charred bovine.

“Bones?” She retracted her smile, trying to ignore the tingle that rushed through her leg as he touched it. “That pinch did not touch bone or fat. That was pure muscle, my friend.” She ate another dipped fry. “Don’t mess with me.” She warned. “I’m too happy with my fries.” The distinctive Cajun seasoning took her back to her happy place. The place locked in her fading memory was precious to her. It was one of the few places where she could remember her mom alive and her dad... normal. Looking off past her fries, Isabel sighed. "You know, my mom used to try to order something different every time we came here. She even got the grilled Cajun catfish one time. It was so gross." Isabel scrunched her nose and smiled.

Jordan put down the remainder of his burger and watched her reminisce. He thought she was most attractive when she was happy. "Was she pretty?" He prodded. It was rare that Isabel would talk about her family, so Jordan wanted to open her up as much as possible.

She nodded with all of her seriousness. "Yeah, she was beautiful. I don't know. I thought she was beautiful." Isabel picked up a fry and just stared at it. She was tired of thinking about her family and all of the mess that came with them. She was exhausted at the thought of her mother. She was done thinking about her father. Of all the things she was ready for in her life, at that moment, even digesting a limp fry seemed much too strenuous a task for her to attempt.

As he watched her mentally dive into the basis of her neurosis, Jordan tried his best to distract his friend. Eating the heavily mayonnaise-drenched fry dangling from Isabel's fingers seemed to be the only distraction that would prove effective enough. In one bite, the spicy, warm fried potato filled his mouth. He tried to swallow the mayonnaise as quickly as he could, and as a result, choked himself hoarse. With watery eyes, Jordan forced out words. "Oh man, Bel. That was gross."

The payoff came when she began to laugh at him wiping away the condensation from his eyes. "Drink some water." She passed him her water with lime. "You didn't have to swallow it in one gulp."

She lectured him as he sucked down half the glass. "Next time try chewing first."

Finally Jordan cleared all fry and mayonnaise residue from his throat, knocking his foot against Isabel's for companionship. He smirked sideways to her as he sipped a little more water. "Now you know why you married me." Closing his eyes and dimpling in his right cheek, Jordan had successfully diverted her attention.

"That's why? I want a divorce." She lightly tapped his foot as she ate another fry.

The dimple faded into an expression of disdain. "Judas? Who names their kid Judas?" He thought aloud. "Maybe Jude, but Judas? All he needs is to find a nice girl named Jezebel, and he'll be all set." Slowly his dimple began to return. "See? You can't date him. Wrong name."

She rolled her eyes as they embarked on an hour's worth of barely platonic banter. By the end of their meal, Isabel had eaten three baskets of fries and more mayonnaise than most people would eat in two weeks. Jordan's arm remained stretched out behind her to keep her close to him. "So now what do you want to do?" He asked as she ingested her last fry.

"Now we... oh wait! What time is it?" She grabbed his wrist that lay behind her so that she could look at his watch. "Oh, man! It's one o'clock. There used to be a drive-in that usually had a midnight showing. I wanted to see if it was still in business. Rats!" She set his wrist back behind her. "You know, if we weren't such tired old people, we could see if there were any clubs going."

"If." Jordan was never up for the club scene. He flagged down the waiter. "Could we have the check, please?" They both waited for the bitter response they had quickly grown accustomed to, but were pleasantly disappointed by a polite nod.

When he came back with their bill, Isabel spoke up as Jordan fished through his wallet. "Besides clubs, what else is there to do around here at night?"

Without being invited, he sat in the booth seat across from Isabel and Jordan, stunning them both. "Well, Isabel," he rhymed on purpose, "clubs are really all there is around here. The jazz one on twenty-fifth is the best. You could walk in Hetzel's Park. There's not much else to do there. Do you know where Hetzel's is, Isabel?" He asked her. She nodded in response as Jordan ignored them both and slid the bill and cash to Judas. "Hetzel's is your best bet. Although, it's a full moon out tonight." His eyes fully focused on Isabel's face as he picked up the money and bill, causing Isabel to blush a bright shade of embarrassed pink. "I'll be right back with your change, guys."

Jordan and Isabel looked at each other as though they weren't sure what to do with this strange waiter. "You want him. You know it." Jordan scooted her out of the booth. "He's mean to you, so now you're going to want him." He concluded, leaving no room for a reply. Before she could think of a valid protest, Judas had come back with their change. He rested the five dollars and twenty-seven cents on the table, glancing at Isabel with a mild look of dislike. "Have a good night." He tossed at them.

Deciding it best not to comment back, Isabel reluctantly looked up at Jordan to prove that she was not attracted to men who are rude to her. Slapping his hands together, Jordan was ready to go. "Come on, kid. Let's go home. I'm getting tired." He turned his back to her and slightly bent his knees.

"Hop on." He smiled, pointing his thumb towards his back.

With a large, not so graceful leap, Isabel stuck herself like Velcro onto his back. Jordan carried her to the car and dumped her in, unlocking her giggles. It was late and they were both starting to grow tired. As Jordan realized that there was obviously no food in front of him, his mouth began to feel very lonely, and his lips felt empty. He began to wish for the woman in the red shirt again.

"Turn right. It's just a mile up the road... I think on the left is the freeway." She pointed out the window. No matter how hard she tried to focus on Grille24 or navigating the way home, she could not shake the image of him smoking and not even telling her about it. Against her better judgment, she let frustration get the better of her. Breathing heavily, she lowered her eyes. "So, were you going to tell me that you've started smoking again?" She asked in one breath. "Or is that the kind of information only that woman at the restaurant is privy to?"

Jordan cleared his throat as he searched for some way out of the argument he knew was about to take over. "How long have you known?" He asked, kicking himself the moment the words escaped his mouth.

Isabel gaped at his response to being caught. "How long has this been going on? How long have you been sneaking around? Were you ever going to tell me? Your best friend?" She shook her head and stared out the window. "Well?" She prodded indignantly.

The steam built up inside of Jordan as he tried to search for the right thing to say. "Bel, I didn't say anything to anyone because I don't want to be smoking. You were the last person I wanted to find out about this."

"Well, I guess that's obvious, being that a complete stranger knew before I caught you. Why couldn't you just tell me? I can help you."

For the first time in minutes, Jordan craned his head to look at her directly. "Is this you helping me? Gee, I wonder why I was thinking you would flip out. You're just handling the disappointment so well now." He shook his head. "Does it bother you that you are entirely predictable?" He knew that he should not have taken the argument to this level, but he was not going to hold back now.

"That is not fair!" Isabel shrieked. "You sneak around, lie to me for who knows how long, and I'm the bad guy because you're destroying your body? That's great Jordan. Do you need another cigarette? Because I think the fresh air is going to your head."

"Guess what, Bel? I'm stressed out. I'm having a problem with this. I can't quit." He enunciated every syllable. "I should have known that you would do this. First you did it to Donny, and now me."

"Geez, Jordan. Don't go there. What exactly did I do to Donny? Make him cheat on me? Tell me about my relationship that you know nothing about." She warned as she looked out the window at the three empty lanes on their right.

"I don't have to know all about you and Donny to know what happened. You were happy with him until one day you decided to branch out on your own for no apparent reason. When he didn't understand why all of a sudden you wouldn't hold his hand in public, why you pulled away when he'd try to kiss you, you started looking at him like he was some pathetic loser. Kind of like the way you're looking at me right now." He stated without even having to glance at his friend. "You wouldn't break it off with him, so he hooked up with someone who *would* look at him." Jordan paused, trying to steady his tone. "Somehow he failed to be perfect, so you pushed him away. You saw in him some weakness, and you just couldn't stand the sight of him anymore. We all saw it. If someone steps out of the line you think they should be in, you cut them off." He stated what the boys knew to be obvious. "Does calling out other people's problems make it easier to ignore your own?"

Instead of a bitter retort spewing out from her mouth, Isabel just stared at her friend, eyes wide from the shock of his audacity. No one had ever called her out on her character flaws like this before. She had never expected Jordan to speak to her so harshly. "You know nothing about Donny and me. I do not cut people out of my life." She reached for any rebuttal.

Jordan tried to keep his eyes on the road without gawking at her. "That's what you do, Bel." He brought the obvious fact to the surface for her to confront. "You stuff people into boxes and throw them away when they don't fit inside." He accurately summed up the root of the demise of all of her relationships.

She was shocked that her best friend thought such horrible things about her. Even worse than him thinking them, were they true? For a moment she searched through her immediate past for more traces of this newly unearthed dysfunction. "Jordan, you can't make general statements like that based on one instance - an instance which you know very little about, by the way." She felt the need to remind him. That was the first time her secrecy had actually paid off.

Jordan had not wanted to unleash this mess onto his friend. He had not even thought of discussing it with her. Now that the cat was out of the bag, he traveled on further with his point. "I'm not making general statements. How about the last time I started smoking? You stopped talking to me instead of just, you know, loving me." He had trouble saying the word "love" when it came to their friendship, and always thought it through long before it actually came out of his mouth. He labeled that as such a delicate word, which made it all the more difficult to put it on someone like her, who was known to be reckless with other people's hearts.

To cover up the "L" word, Jordan rushed on. "When Geoff failed one of his finals senior year, the first thing out of your mouth was criticism. You told him that he should have studied harder. Do you know how badly that hurt him? You put people on this pedestal, and if they even glance down from it you get all rattled, like it's a personal attack on you or something." Jordan held his next example on his tongue so as to stop from beating her with his point. "You're like, my best friend in the world, and even I know that I will never measure up to the person you have me built up to be in your mind." Jordan took a long breath. "The scary part about that thought is that I know you better than anyone (other than maybe your brother), but I have to make sure you don't know all of me so that you don't one day just decide to stop talking to me because I smoke, or I do some stupid thing that I'm tired of hiding from you." He had not meant to hurt her feelings. He was perfectly willing to be partially unknown by his best friend. He just wanted her to be happy, which he was usually good at accomplishing in her.

The only noise now was the slight whirring of air whipping against the outside of the windows. Jordan could feel her tension, and quickly tried to come around to a sensible conclusion. "Eesa, I'm not trying to make you feel like a bad person or hurt your feelings. I just want you to see all of this as it is. Maybe then you could let go of some of that anger you bark at your brother. Maybe you would smile more. I don't know," Jordan reached for the one thing he was trying not to say. "Maybe you could see your dad for who he really was. Maybe he wouldn't seem so horrible to you then."

Though she was able to tolerate listening to Jordan talk about all of her wrong choices, she was not prepared for the low blow father card. "You had to go there, didn't you?" She shook her head. "Don't you talk to me about him. You have no idea what all of that was, and what it still is. You know, I can take other people giving me their advice and telling me that they understand. What I can't handle is hearing all that bull from you. What authority do you have to even suggest something? You have never even met the man. You didn't know him before my mom died, and you didn't know him after. You will never know him now, and the world is a better place now that he's not in it." Her hateful words shook her insides, causing her to quake visibly.

"Bel, this is what I'm talking about. You put people in a box. You always talk about him like he is just that one guy. You forget that he's also the guy who loved your mom. You completely disregard that he's also the guy who took his family to Grille24 every week and let his wife order whatever she wanted. It's okay to be mad at him. If he weren't dead and I met him, I may have killed him for being that second guy. You're forgetting that once upon a time you loved him as that first guy." Jordan pushed further into the mess, causing Isabel to grind her teeth to keep from welling up. "Granted, he took a pretty far leap from that box of perfection you had him in, but Bel, no matter what the crime, he never would have fit into it. Nobody can live up to their box. People are not perfectly white, and while you know that, what you fail to see is that no one is completely black either. When your father did what he did to you, it did not make him a clearly cut bad guy. It made him your dad who needed to go to jail and get some help. It did not negate every kind thing he had ever done before that point."

All of Isabel's muscles were tightened so much that she squirmed in her seat, hoping that all of her capped anger would not make her body implode. As Jordan paused to collect his thoughts, Isabel fought for control over her words. "Do not defend him to me." She spat out. "Even the judge saw him as a bad guy. It wasn't my *box* or *labels* that made him do that." She clawed at her jeans to keep from screaming out her anger.

"You missed my point, Bel." Jordan corrected her, increasing his speed. "It was him who did all of those things. No one suggested any of that to him, least of all you. I'm just saying that he is *more* than those things. He was your dad. Man, you're so afraid to be sad because then you'll have to admit that his death may be something to be sad about. You won't even let yourself think about who he was before all of this. If you put him in the bad guy box, then you understand him as being just that, and you can dismiss him because he's just a bad guy. Isabel, no one is that simple. Your father was not totally good or totally bad. He wasn't black or white. No one is! We're all just different shades of gray. Even the lightest shade of gray has a little bit of black in it. Your dad, as dark as what he did was, I bet there were still lots of times in his life that he made you smile." Jordan sighed and silently wished that he could take back all of the callous things he was saying to her. "I don't know why you are so afraid to be sad or conflicted or feel anything about him. It doesn't matter if you fall apart for a little while. You have three people and a whole huge family to help you put all the pieces back together. By only letting him be the bad guy in your mind, all you're doing is holding the poison inside of you longer. You don't have to forgive your dad, or anyone else for that matter. But if you don't let people be gray, then you will end up alone, and no one will be there when you decide to let yourself finally feel something. I can only hold you together for so long, Eesa. When are you going to make an effort to take care of yourself? You push me out, and then what? You are so far in denial, that you can't even see how much we have to do for you because you can't do it for yourself. I pray that you don't cut me off for this. Not for my sake, but for yours. You're a mess, and you don't even see it."

For several minutes neither friend made an effort to speak. They both unwillingly sat next to each other, processing the entire conversation. After a prolonged period of tension, the low hum of the wind began to relax them. Isabel made the first move by opening her window and letting the breezy night air seep in. The air was beginning to smell different, as the seasons were just starting to change. "Get onto 75." Isabel spoke, feeling weighed down by their discussion.

Without a word, they drove home with visible distance between them. Hours of silence passed before they reached their destination. Even as they walked up the steps to their apartments, they did not speak to each other. Rusty wheels began to turn in Isabel's tired brain, and finally something clicked. She turned to her friend just before he disappeared behind his door. "Jordan." She made sure to keep her voice low.

He was shocked that she had spoken to him, and turned at once. "Yeah?"

"Can I borrow your car?" She asked with her eyebrows pushing themselves together.

While Jordan's answer was usually a firm and assertive "no", at that moment he would have given her anything to erase the permanent words he had pushed on her that night. "Okay. Where are you going?" He whispered, stepping back out into the hallway.

"I'm not sure. I just don't want to be here." She leaned against the wall next to her door. "I just want to go for a drive." Her gaze was aimed downward, so that she would not have to look at him.

"Let me take you." He offered, but when she shook her head, still staring at her shoes, his controlled façade broke. "I'm so sorry, Bel." It was all he could think to say. Even as she resisted it, he reached out and touched her face. "I shouldn't have brought this all up now. It's clearly not the right time to do this, with the viewing being tomorrow." When she still did not say anything to him, he kept on. "Talk to me. How can I fix this?"

Isabel blinked as she heard that trigger word. "You can't." She turned her head away from his hand. "RJ said the same thing today. I thought he was just being RJ, but what if he's right? Am I making you all miserable?" She questioned as she stood up straight. "I don't want to be the one who can't take care of herself. I don't want to wake everyone up at night. I don't want to always rely on all three of you to fix me. You were both right. *I* need to fix me. Something is wrong, and I need to figure out what to do about it." She shook her head and began nervously scratching her collarbone. "So can I just have the keys?" Looking up at her dumbfounded friend, her dark eyes pleaded with him to let her go.

Against his better judgment, Jordan handed her the keys to his car. "Okay, Bel. Do you have your cell phone?" He questioned, knowing that he would not sleep well with her on the road all night. She checked her pocket and nodded. "RJ's going to kill me, you realize. Try to be back before he wakes up."

Isabel pulled away from the hand that was still resting on her and left without saying goodbye. Jordan was at a loss as to what was the right thing to do. Usually when she needed to be fixed, he would just hold her until she felt better. His strong arms felt incredibly useless and weak as he watched her disappear down the stairs. A whisper of intense loneliness crept upon him as the realization finally hit him that after tonight, she might not need him anymore. Turning to his apartment, he went straight to his bedroom and lay down on top of his sheets. Of course he had wanted her to deal with her father. Of course he had wanted her to eat normal food without being told. Of course he wanted her to sleep peacefully through the night. He just never thought she would actually do it. Now she was out in the night, alone, dealing with things for the first time, and he was stuck in his apartment playing the dreaded waiting game.

Isabel started up the coveted car and pulled out, not sure where she was going. She knew that she had to think about things that she had worked very hard to erase from her memory. There was only one person that she could talk to who would listen and let her come to a rational conclusion that was sure to be her own. She turned the corner and drove towards the spot where Homeless Joe always sat. Parking a few yards before she reached his spot, Isabel got out and stretched her torso. Craning her neck to look ahead, Isabel saw an unusual sight. Next to the familiar lamppost lay nothing but empty cement. Isabel gasped. Surely she had been mistaken. Quickly blinking twice, she checked again.

Still the cement was empty. "Joe?" She called out in what felt like a yell, but what was really a yelp. In shock, her eyes locked on the empty cement. She began whimpering as she ran to the empty spot, hoping that maybe the man was perhaps hiding behind the thin lamppost. "He's not here." She spoke to no one but herself. The world grew increasingly dimmer as she shuddered. "Two years... always here... Joe? Joe?" She repeated his name in a way that made her voice crack. Over and over she spoke his name, speaking as though she were present in her own nightmare. "Joe? Joe?" Her eyes were as big as silver dollars with salty tears forming tiny pools in her eyes.

She stopped herself from the tears that were breaking the surface as she double and triple checked that this was in fact, the right spot. She tried to stay calm, even though she knew that this would impact her more than she could control. Without waiting for the tears to come, she pulled herself down the street. *Maybe he just went for a walk.* She thought, as she looked around frantically for him. She passed a used bookstore, three small restaurants, and several clothing stores with no sign of Joe. With every step she took, Isabel had to wrestle with the thought that she would not find her friend. Now it seemed necessary to search the streets for a nameless homeless man.

For nearly twenty minutes she searched Homeless Joe's street and the surrounding streets with no reward. Isabel had let go of her pride and allowed herself to go through every stage of crying by the time she had finally declared him gone. When she crawled back into the car, her sobs had simmered to mere sniffles. He was gone. For no reason at all, he had left her life. Isabel fought the urge to sit by the lamppost and wait for him to return. She understood that he would not come back to her, and that thought flashed as a complete sentence in her mind. The bun wound tightly on top of her head had partially unraveled, leaving stray strands of black hair hanging in her face and around her cold neck. She missed Jordan and craved to be in his arms, but refused to make the phone call to wake him up. To keep her fingers from dialing him, she turned her cell phone off. This was just one more thing that she would do on her own, she decided.

Her tears were gone, as was the bold look of denial she had been masking since her father had died. Replacing her forced bravery was a look of bleak depression. Instead of being coddled and held, Isabel stood alone. She came to the conclusion that no amount of babying would make her cope better. For the entirety of two long hours she stared at the steering wheel, conjuring up dark memories that she had effortlessly kept in the dark for so long.

Her life played like a silent movie in her brain, only bringing up a few clips that had not been completely buried. Tears squeezed out of her clenched shut-eyes as she recalled a childhood she would just as soon have forgotten. M*om taking me to ballet class... My four goldfish that dad bought me... A birthday party, probably my tenth birthday... RJ's pet frog that he named "The Flash"... Grille24... Dad telling a joke about... about... what? What was the joke?* The invisible filmstrip stopped as Isabel tried to remember the joke that she recalled her father telling with such enthusiasm. As she pictured him telling the joke, he did not look sinister to her. He did not look drunk. She had forgotten what he had looked like before her mom had died. He smiled a lot and was always telling them stories about the guys at work. In that specific memory, he did not look like such a bad guy. She dug even deeper and remembered that in this memory, she was happy to be with her dad, not afraid.

Isabel shuddered, as she did not know what to do with this new layer she had peeled off of her father. *So was he this nice guy who went bad? He couldn't have been a rapist for fifteen years before it finally came out. If you're a rapist at the end of your life, does that mean that you always were? Or does it mean that he just changed drastically midway through his life? Can one year of your life define who you are completely? Why would anyone morph into a rapist when their wife dies? Was she just holding him back all those years? No, no. You can't hide a secret from your family for fifteen years.* Isabel strained every ounce of her mental power to come up with a clear answer. As no clarity came to her, she proceeded to bang her head against the steering wheel until all of the conflicting thoughts stopped. When her mind stopped swirling around hypothesizing the reasons of her father's demise, everything became very still around her. She could hear no rustling from the streets or wind blowing outside the car. As her head rested, frozen on the steering wheel, one concise, clear thought surfaced within her. *None of that matters. My dad is dead, and that is sad.* The idea stamped itself permanently to her forehead.

Slowly picking up her head, Isabel came back to life. She had made a decision. She had figured out how she felt about her father's death. Even though she decided to be sad that her dad had died, that thought brought about such peace and contentment. She almost smiled at the closure that was seeping in all around her, coloring in the emptiness that she had been using the boys to fill. A sigh expelled out of her lungs that emptied out the grudges she had been holding inside of her. As they dissipated out of her body, she was amazed at how much lighter she felt. She had not noticed that she had been living her life with thirty pounds of dead weight on her back. To finally have unbuckled the burden was incredibly elating. More satisfying to her, though, was the fact that she had unbuckled it herself.

Without even bothering to check behind her for other drivers, Isabel peeled out of the parking space, lucky not to hit anyone. Faster than she had ever sped before, she drove towards the familiar cemetery with the windows rolled all the way down. Although she was freezing and her knuckles felt like they were frosted onto the steering wheel, she had never felt more alive.

For once she did not allow her wounded, bitter self to dwell in her heart, but rather embraced whatever peace she could gather. Jordan had been right to say that no person could be completely awful. Even though her father had died with no reconciliation attempted by either side, her lengthy memory could still manage to stretch back to at least one time that she loved him. As she drove to her new destination, one more pure memory had surfaced from where she had kept it safely buried. She recalled how her father used to mow the grass every Saturday morning, whether it needed it or not. Isabel would look out of her window on the first day of the weekend, and see him out working on the lawn. Her mother would always chastise him for using his favorite, rackety old push mower when they could buy a new self-propelled one, or that they could even hire someone to do it. She even tried to buy him a new one for Christmas one year, but it just sat in the garage because he refused to use it. When he would come in from his hours spent pushing the old lawn mower, he would be covered in damp grass blades from his waist down, and no one could come near him without getting dirty. When her mother would tell him to take his filthy shoes off before coming into the house, he would just ignore her directions and run around the house to give her a wild kiss, covering her in the grass as well.

Isabel smiled to herself as the tears gushed out of her. She flew to the cemetery, ignoring the speed limit signs. When she reached the town her mother was buried in, she searched for a twenty-four hour superstore to pick up a few essentials she had thought of on her way there. Not bothering with social protocol, she ran through the huge store to the home and garden section. Quickly picking a small trowel from one of the shelves, she then sought out a perfect pot of flowers that she could plant by the two graves. The most beautiful ones there were yellow mums and red mums. She took one pot of each and quickly paid so that she could complete her mission before sunrise.

She drove to the dimly lit cemetery, knowing that she would be the only one there. As she crept by in Jordan's car, she tried to remember just exactly where her mother's grave was located. Finally seeing the familiar tombstone sticking up out of the ground, she parked her car and walked with pots and trowel in hand to her mother.

A small tingle swept over her shoulders as she approached her mother's headstone. Right next to it was the spot dug out for her father, where tomorrow he would be freshly buried in the tossed earth. While her mother's stone went up to Isabel's knees and had a beautiful poem inscribed on it, she knew that her father's would receive no such accolade. She imagined that he would probably have a small slab that had his name and lifespan carved in it. Possibly even a “Rest in Peace”, which Isabel did not think would be possible for her father.

It took a few minutes of staring at the sad tombstone before she remembered what she had come there to do. Disregarding the fact that she was wearing her favorite jeans, Isabel knelt onto the ground and began to plant the flowers. As she was not familiar with this process, it took her a while to pick the flowers up out of the pot without disturbing the roots. Digging the small hole in the ground gave her the sensation of digging her parents up out of the earth. Even though her father's body was resting at the funeral home, she still envisioned that he was lying just a few feet beneath her, begging his daughter to release him from the earth. Her arms moved faster, and she did not seem to care that her spotless red sweater now had dirt caked onto the sleeves. With every scoop of dirt that lifted, she hoped to unearth one of her parents. Either one of them could have righted so much of the wrong that had shaken her world. When she finally realized that no one would ever come back to her, she began to cry anew. She did not stop her digging, but rather let her tears fall freely on her mother, letting them both know how much she wanted her back. After several minutes of fitful digging, she realized that she had dug a hole much too big for the plants. Slowly, she put some of the dirt back in, her chin quivering as she felt the heavy responsibility of burying her parents.

In the quietness of the cemetery, she allowed her father to be the man that she loved. She began to cry with her father for her mother who had died. Her mother who had left their lives so prematurely would have wanted them to mourn as a family, so Isabel allowed her tears remain, as her mother would have wanted. Her large, salty tears dripped over the freshly planted flowers as she cried for her mother. As she openly wept for her mother, she was comforted by being able to cry with her father. She never let herself remember how much she missed the sane version of him. It was much too hurtful to let herself see him without all of his glaring misdeeds. That night had left her open to floods of feelings that she had gladly been living without. For the next hour, she cried while sitting atop of her parents, missing them sorely.

When she had finally drained herself of tears, she picked herself up off of the cold ground and wiped her face with the dirt-stained sleeve. Slowly she gathered the pot and trowel, throwing them away in the open garbage can in the middle of the cemetery. Making sure to dust as much of the dirt off as she could, she then sat in Jordan's clean car. The sun was beginning to creep up over the horizon, reminding her that she needed to go home.

Making sure to fill up the gas tank before she reached the apartment, Isabel tiptoed quietly up the stairs and unlocked her door. Her plan to not wake up RJ was foiled the moment she entered the living room and saw him sitting on the couch. He glanced up and gaped at her. "Where have you been?" He barked, staring at his dirt-spattered sister. He had assumed that Isabel had slept in Jordan's room that night, but when he saw Jordan and no Isabel, he panicked. Jordan had assured him that she had just gone out to blow off a little steam, that she would be fine. To see her so dirty and disheveled was quite a shock.

Isabel inhaled deeply and calmly explained that she had gone for a drive. "I'm fine, RJ. Really." She offered. "I went to see mom and dad's burial plot, that's all." She glanced at her watch and saw that it was almost time for her to leave for work. "I've actually got to get in the shower now though, I have to be at work in a little bit." She walked towards the bathroom.

"Eesa, I called Max and told him that you wouldn't be in today or tomorrow." RJ stood up off of the couch and walked towards her. "And never, *never* go out like that again with your phone turned off. I could kill Jordan!" He shouted at her.

Isabel stopped and turned to stare at her brother. "RJ, why would you call Max? Weren't you the one who gave me the speech about taking care of myself? How am I supposed to do that with you making all of my decisions for me? Trust me, I'm fine. I am going to work today. I'll see you when you get home." She shut herself in the bathroom and turned on the water before he could think up a decent rebuttal.

As RJ was too shocked to be rational, he hurried over to the boys' apartment, finding Jordan watching television on the couch. "Isabel was out all night!" He confessed to Jordan. "Now she's going to work all day. You were supposed to watch her!" He cried out the betrayal.

Jordan watched his friend and waited for RJ to explain why Isabel going to work was a problem. At any moment, RJ looked as though the stress would overtake him. "Just, will you just watch her today at least? Take her out today. Go see one of those awful movies with the subtitles she likes. Here." He pulled a wad of cash from his wallet and shoved it at Jordan. "Just make sure she's okay."

The money being thrust at him showed Jordan just how desperate RJ was. Polite and speaking calmly, Jordan pushed the money away. "RJ, I don't need money. We work at the same place." He looked his worried friend directly in the eye. "She will be fine. She's twenty-five years old. No one needs to babysit her. She is not going to leave you."

"But I really need – " RJ borderline pleaded his nonessential case.

"RJ." This was one of the few times in his life where he was RJ's superior. The steady upper hand guided him through the forceful conversation. "Get going to the viewing. She'll be fine. Go out with your family afterwards. Hang out with Geoff. Make out with that girl you were out with yesterday. Get out of here and do what you need to do. Isabel will be just fine." Jordan spelled out the command, leaving little room for argument, and pointed his arm to the door.

As the wheels turned in RJ's head, Jordan hoped that he had not overstepped his boundaries. RJ postured and clenched his fits as though he would like nothing better than to physically fight with Jordan, as he wasn't winning the verbal fight. "You'd better watch her this time." For the first time ever witnessed by Jordan, RJ surprised both of them. He backed down. "Tell Geoff I'm in my room." Still fuming from the fight, RJ left the apartment.

Jordan showered and dressed quietly so that Geoff could be awakened by his deafening alarm clock. Geoff had only just fallen asleep a few hours before his alarm clock blared in his ears. Work was slowly beginning to take its toll on Geoff. The consecutive shifts were starting to wear on his senses, causing his morning routine to retard slightly. Geoff was usually a cheerful morning person. While most people were fully roused by their shower, Geoff was awake and chipper seconds after his alarm rang. Today however, his morning song and dance (and whistle) would not start until after his lukewarm shower and scalding hot coffee with milk and three teaspoons of sugar. His eyes were still hardly opened, and he could barely focus on stirring his coffee. As his mind was slowly beginning to pick up speed, he noticed a napkin laid out on the counter in front of his favorite "Don't touch my coffee" mug. A short note was scribbled in Isabel's loopy, seventh grade handwriting.

Geoff flattened out the napkin on the counter and read over the note Isabel had left for him. As Jordan emerged from his bedroom, a high, lofty whistle sneaked across his lips as Jordan sat down and flipped through the channels on the television. "So, where'd you two get off to last night?" He studied his roommate's reactions carefully.

Jordan did not even look up from the colorful screen to answer Geoff's subtle hinting. "We went to this restaurant she used to go to with her family when she was younger." Jordan allowed himself to smile over that little gem. "Did you know she eats fries with mayonnaise on them?" Jordan tore his eyes away from the television to glance over at Geoff.

"Wow. Sorry I missed that. That's much better than just eating jam." He sipped his coffee without an ounce of sincerity in his voice. "So what are you going to do today with Isabel at work?" His coffee was slowly beginning to cool down. Geoff was well aware that there was a ten-minute window in which he could drink his coffee without it being too hot or too cold.

"I don't know. RJ wants me to keep an eye on her today." He cracked his tender knee joints as he stood.

Geoff raised his eyebrows. "Well, your day sounds much more fun than mine. Want to trade? You can go see the dead rapist, and I'll pretend to hang out with Isabel." He tossed as he downed the rest of his coffee. He left his roommate and began brushing his teeth and completing other menial morning missions. "Hey Jordan, can you tie this?"

He balled up one of his three ties and tossed it at his couch-slouched friend. Ties took a great deal of time and patience for Geoff to master, while Jordan could tie the perfect Windsor knot with his eyes closed. Within seconds, the tie was twisted perfectly and hooked onto the owner's neck. "Thanks. I have to go." He grabbed his phone and coat, exiting out to the next apartment.

Jordan followed behind his friend to the apartment across the hall. "Eesa, do you need a ride to work?" He called at her bedroom.

"Yes!" She emerged, looking frazzled. "I'm leaving, RJ." She twisted up her long, wet hair into a tight bun, which could never seem to stay where she wanted it. As she put on her coat, she kissed Geoff's cheek. "You're a hero for doing this, you know. He's just awful today."

Smiling down at his friend, he noticed that she looked a little bit different to him. He could not quite put his finger on it, but something had definitely changed in her. "Yeah, well, by day, hero, by night, ordinary male nurse." He buttoned the top button of her coat and kissed her forehead. "Come on, RJ." He beckoned his friend to the hallway. RJ stalked out of the apartment, not bothering to shut the door on his way out.

Isabel had been waiting for a moment alone with Jordan. "I'm sorry about last night." She confessed. "I took your car to see my mom's tombstone. I just needed to do some thinking." She kept her voice low so that if the two boys were still lingering in the hall, they would not hear her.

Last night he had been so scared that he had pushed her too hard. Letting her drive off in his car all night did not help to calm his fears either. Seeing her that morning, looking relatively happy to see him caused the breath he was holding in to expel out of his lungs.

"You know I love you, right?" She searched his eyes to silently communicate all of the things that those words meant.

Jordan's heart swelled and he could not stop from kissing her cheeks several times. "Yes." He held her face and kissed her forehead. "I love you, Bel." He confessed.

Closer than she felt she ever had before, she held him. The hug, filled with all of its momentum, possessed a certain healing power that they both desperately needed. Their stomachs fit tightly to each other as their bodies would not dare to leave the other one. Cheek to cheek, they clung together in a hug dripping with the urgency of both of their deeply hidden longings for each other. “Jordan, I...” Isabel whispered, taking the time to softly kiss Jordan’s jaw. She could not bring herself to finish the sentence. To keep herself from saying things that neither of them could utter, she buried herself into his firm chest and allowed his arms to encircle her. Staying in the safe haven for several moments, she closed her eyes and pressed her ear to his heart, knowing full well how strong it was. Listening to the methodical rhythm of his heartbeat lulled her into a state of total relaxation. After seven beats, she realized that the thud of her own heart was matched up to his, and that thought was encouraging. Knowing that she was passing their normal friendly affections, she kissed his cheek again, letting her lips stay a moment longer than usual. Fearing that she would blurt out things that they felt, but never said, she whispered in his ear, “I crashed your car last night.”

“You know, that’s never funny.” He kissed her cheek and smelled her skin. He pulled back and stole one more kiss from the top of her head, holding her face. Jordan kissed her cheek one more time, wanting more.

"Let's get out of here." He willed his hands to stop touching her face. Taking her by the hand, he cursed himself as he led her out of the apartment.

Chapter Five

Get me out of here was RJ's one protruding thought as he and Geoff entered the cramped funeral home. There was a funeral being held there along with the viewing that day, and the larger crowd of mourners had come to see a woman who died in her eighties by the name of Virginia McAllister. They had arrived much earlier than anyone else, and were the only people in the building not mourning the death of dear, sweet Virginia. An anxious RJ peered into the smaller parlor marked for Richard Scillio as Geoff busied himself signing the guestbook for the both of them. RJ loathed wearing his tie in this particular setting, as it was beginning to feel more like a noose every minute. For the seventh time since they had arrived, RJ tugged at his black and green tie. The coffin was the focus of the dimly lit room, with only one bouquet of red and white carnations to send their condolences. Frozen to stone, RJ stood, staring at the closed casket. He had not considered a closed casket, which he preferred. He had gone for his usual run that morning, but his missing sister and preparing himself to see his father for the last time clouded his mind. The realization that he now did not have to see anything but the casket relaxed his tensed shoulders a bit. The air was still thick though, smelling of dust and old lady makeup. Still frozen in the middle of the maroon carpeted aisle, RJ began to picture his father (whom he had not seen in years) inside of the casket. He lay so still, and RJ imagined that his hands were probably crossed over his chest in the same way that his mother's hands had been laid. The soft velvet would be crushing all around him on every side. The casket closed, leaving no more than an inch of breathing room for his dead father.

Breathing room. RJ found that thought to be terribly ironic as he found the air harder to suck into his own lungs. There would be no more air for his father, he realized. He was unknowingly rotting before his son's very eyes. Though the casket was closed, RJ could see worms crawling all over and through his father's limp body, causing RJ's arm to itch. Brushing the imaginary worm off his shoulder, RJ tried to stay still and face his father for the first time in years. He was probably wearing his old brown suit coat with the tan patches on the elbows. RJ could not help but see that brown suit wrapped around a moldy, grey skeleton in the coffin before him. His skeletal... moldy... worm-infested father. Yes, the air was definitely too heavy to take a full breath. He had to escape.

Turning around, RJ headed for the door he had just entered in from. Geoff, the dutiful friend, had been patiently watching him, and now had concern plastered across his face. RJ hated concern. He was fine, and despised it when anyone else pitied him or acted as though he was not in complete control of the situation. "Don't look at me like that." He growled without meaning to. As his family had not yet arrived at the funeral home, RJ felt less shameful as he hurriedly stalked out to the exit with Geoff trailing at his heels. Without even glancing at the freckle-faced receptionist on his way out, RJ pushed through the heavy double wooden doors and forced his frown upon the sunshine that dared to sparkle outside.

Geoff did not bother to pause or ask questions, he only watched his friend somberly and waited for a sign as to what he should do. RJ's broad chest heaved with the pressure of ten excruciating years. Eventually the sun proved soothing to the now fatherless son. Soon the warmth on his shoulder began to evaporate, along with his need for catharsis. Being away from the dreaded casket relaxed him almost enough to coax his facial muscles to loosen up a bit. It was then that he decided he would rather not be wearing a tie.

Catching his serious friend's suddenly casual demeanor, Geoff joined him in tearing off his tie with all the thrill of a six-year-old boy on Easter Sunday. "I know what you're thinking," he looped his tie around his forehead in true first grade fashion. "But you're wrong. It takes six hundred and three licks to get to the tootsie roll center of a tootsie pop. Not six hundred and two." He stared straight ahead into the parking lot, trying to locate his car.

This was what RJ needed in order to come to terms with the funeral home. Humor was just the ticket to squelch his qualms about leaving. "Liar." He permitted a half-smile and looped his own dangling black and green tie around his forehead to join Geoff's club. He had tried to be in the same room with his father, and for those four and a half minutes it had been nearly bearable. Now he felt the freedom to leave.

Geoff's eyes bulged upon seeing his angrily reserved friend with a tie around his forehead as well. Not wanting to break the momentum, Geoff let go of any notion that they were two tax-paying citizens in their mid-twenties. "Batman never lies." Geoff held his fist out in front of himself to fly to the clean car. He did not want to be there anymore than RJ did. He saw no point in honoring a man who caused as much damage as Mr. Scillio.

"That's Superman! Batman doesn't fly with his fist forward." RJ trotted off after his friend, feeling a bit ridiculous. Sheepishly he removed the tie off of his head as Geoff flew by two sullen mourners. They were two elderly ladies obviously going to see Virginia McAllister. Respectfully, RJ bowed his head to them as he shuffled his feet over to what he was sure was a somewhat deranged version of Geoff. Sitting down in the passenger's seat, RJ threw his tie into the back of the car. "Batman has the grappling hook, but he doesn't fly." He cleared his throat as he clicked his seatbelt.

Peeling out of the respectfully quiet funeral home, Geoff gave RJ his crazy eyes. "There are no downers, workaholics, or boring older brothers allowed in the Batmobile. One more false move and I'll have no choice but to sic Robin on you." He warned as he turned the corner. Now his mission was to have fun with RJ as long as he could push him.

The plan appeared to be working. "You are like, the worst superhero ever!" RJ cried incredulously. Geoff was excited at the difference in RJ. Even if the change were as small as some passionate voice inflection, Geoff would take it. RJ was too caught up in not confining himself to his regular irritating personality to care that he was presently venturing far from it. "Batman would never send Robin in to finish off the bad guy. Robin's just there to do back flips or, I don't know, be used as bait!" He raised his shoulders. "Robin's useless." He nodded his head back and forth smoothly. Glancing at Geoff, he pushed his point so far that some might even have labeled him as ridiculous. Nodding once more, he murmured, "I could take Robin."

Geoff was in his happy place, joking around with the RJ he knew had been lurking somewhere inside. "You dare mock Robin?" Batman questioned as he squealed into a small plaza. "Wait in the car." He opened his door. "Watch out for the Green Goblin." He warned. Geoff was enjoying himself immensely after a full week of worrying and overworking himself. He had not realized how ready he was for a break.

"The Green Goblin's in Spiderman! Man, you suck! Good thing the fate of the universe doesn't rest in your hands." RJ gave up his efforts to control his miniature smile, and gave birth to a full-blown grin. Geoff was his good medicine.

RJ was more open to experiencing fun than he would have been a week ago. Something precious had happened to him that made him forget whom he thought he was supposed to be. Time with Geoff was therapeutic for him, as was time away from home. As he looked in the back at his boring tie, RJ's smile almost disintegrated as thoughts of the funeral home reappeared. Outside of the car, he watched life going on untainted. Gloom settled back in as the superhero rapidly morphed into Eeyore. The car, which sheltered him from the outside world, was used to keep the events of that day (and all of the terrible ones before it) at bay. Grandpa was appropriately respecting his son-in-law's passing. Isabel was going to Grille24 and working - supposedly moving past it. His stomach muscles began to crunch as he questioned to nobody why he was having such a difficult time with all of it. Why he could not even look at his father's casket. Now his old look of determined isolation was etching itself back into his face, filling in the lines left by his previous smile. Maybe he would never understand it. His forlorn mood ground itself into the inner workings of his tender intestines.

The drug store door opened and Geoff was behind it, pushing it open for an attractive redhead. He had a certain weak spot for girls with red hair, which forced him to be a little friendlier than he normally would have been to a stranger in a drug store. She blushed as she walked past the gentleman through the doorway. Looking over her tight-sleeved shoulder, she waved. "Call me." Then she disappeared into her dusty blue escort. If RJ had felt like feeling, he would have been sorry for the poor girl who would never receive the coveted phone call. Unfortunately, RJ remained unmoved as Geoff slid into his vehicle. He threw his brown convenient store bag onto the floor of the back seat and clicked the cold seatbelt over his lap.

With a secretive smile, Geoff backed the car out and drove around to the poorly marked parking lot exit. "Jordan started smoking again, but he doesn't know that I know." He turned right onto the street leading to the freeway.

"Seriously?" RJ shifted in his seat. He had not noticed Jordan acting too abnormally. However, his eyes did not spend their precious time following Jordan around day and night. He felt a small amount of guilt for yelling at him earlier.

Geoff nodded and reached behind him into the bag, pulling out a blue sucker. "Want one?" He pointed it to RJ.

His face mildly scrunching, RJ declined. "No, thanks. I'm twenty-seven." He offered his brief explanation.

Rolling his eyes at good old boring RJ, Geoff unwrapped the sucker, then thought twice and wrapped it back up. "Later." He waved the sucker as he placed it into the cup rest. "I need to sit down when I eat it so that I can keep count."

"You're not serious." RJ had clearly underestimated his friend.

"I was joking at first, but now I'm really curious. I mean, how many licks does it take?" He grinned.

RJ reached back and pulled out the heavy brown bag. "You bought a whole bag full of suckers?"

"Some are for me. I know Isabel will count with me, but the rest are to mess with Jordan. I don't know how long his smoking has been going on, but I found cigarettes in his *secret* hiding spot last night when he was out with Bel. I'm going to replace his cigarette stash with these suckers. I bought that nicotine gum too. I think I'll put that where he keeps the mouthwash. Pretty genius, don't you think?" Geoff raised one light brown eyebrow to show that he was quite pleased with himself.

RJ sighed, trying to act as though he were exasperated with Geoff's behavior. "Don't start something with him. He's real touchy about his smoking." He tried not to be intrigued by Geoff's obviously brilliant evil plan. Just imagining Jordan pulling out the suckers instead of the cigarettes made his eyes almost reveal the good humor that lurked inside of him.

Shifting in his seat, RJ's conscience slowly stirred within him. So rarely did this occur that it took him a moment to reacquaint himself with his estranged better half. "Geoff?" He spoke, still conflicted. "Here's a question." He stalled as he searched for the appropriate words.

"Yeah?" The devious superhero put his pretend cape aside, as he sensed that the subject matter was important.

"Why do you do that to girls?" The image of the blushing redhead rang out in his mind. "Do you ever call them?"

His green eyes grew wide, shocked at RJ's gumption. Since when did RJ pay attention to anything – namely nameless girls? Excuses flooded his brain, clouding an actual response. "Uh, I don't know." He unbuttoned the collar button on his crisp blue dress shirt. "Why do you all of a sudden care?"

Not expecting the conversation to be turned around to him, RJ searched for the root of his newly formed conscience. "I don't." He avoided looking in the general direction of his friend, a little embarrassed that he had put Geoff on the spot.

"Are you going to call that blonde you met?" He tried hard to recall her name. "Adela?" Geoff asked defiantly, not wishing his behavior to be scrutinized.

A gust of air came out of RJ's mouth. "Yeah. I practically begged her for her number."

Geoff smirked as he switched his vehicle over to the middle lane. "You begged?" A mental picture surfaced of RJ clinging to Adela's feet, crying like a baby. That image left Geoff quite satisfied, so he forgave RJ for the personal intrusion and considered RJ's comment.

RJ stared at Geoff coldly. "Yes, I begged. I like her. Do you even like any of these women that you get numbers from?" RJ caught a hold of his composure and closed his mouth.

"Wow. Who knew *you* would harp on me about women? You, of all people." He spoke mostly to himself. In an effort to alleviate some of the tension of the conversation, Geoff consented to searching his motives with women. "RJ, I haven't met my Adela. I'm not looking for her. I don't want to get married like half of the women my age are looking to do. I don't want a serious relationship. I don't even want a second date." He paused to think through his next set of confessions. "You're right. I shouldn't take their phone numbers when I have no intention of calling. Really, I just think it's more fun to date around than to be tied down to one woman, you know? Who invented the concept of one woman? I never tell them I'm interested in monogamy. They just see what they want to see."

"Polygamy? Come on, Geoff." RJ tried to focus his friend on the actual issue. "Have you ever called a girl back for a second date?"

Geoff swallowed and shifted in his seat uncomfortably. "I don't know."

"Then why take their number? Why make them think you'll call?" RJ suddenly began to think about all of the random women whose business cards and scribbled cell phone numbers ended up in the bottom of the garbage can. He did not know why he cared, and frankly it felt foreign for him to show such concern over strangers. In the back of his mind, he was picturing Adela waiting by the phone for some guy like Geoff to call. His countenance saddened as he imagined how crushed she would feel if that had ever happened to her.

"I don't know, RJ. Why do you close yourself off from your closest friends and your family? How often do you even date?" He felt defensive and needed to turn the conversation.

RJ honestly thought through Geoff's frantic questions. Self-awareness was not exactly his strong suit. Luckily, he had a verbally uninhibited sister who had a knack for putting him in his place. "Isabel always tells me that I don't want to let people know me."

"Exactly. That's why I don't call back." Geoff sighed, obviously feeling pressured. "Man, RJ." His eyes darted around on the road, hating and not really understanding the recklessness that drove him to say his next piece. "The only woman I've ever wanted to know me was your sister."

Neither man spoke for several minutes. RJ finally looked over at Geoff, as the superhero wiped the newly formed sweat off of his palms. "And I think we both know how that turned out." He chuckled nervously. "I introduced her to my best friend (who just happened to be the person she's supposed to be with), and unknowingly left myself to pursue the rest of the women of the world." A forced cocky smile broke the sadness of the conversation. Geoff thought far back to when he had eyes for RJ's baby sister. "So far I have yet to meet a woman I can love as much as ..." He cleared his throat to conclude this all too honest thought. "...Jordan loves her. She's better off." Now he had finished investing his emotions in painfully reminiscing.

For many moments both men did not speak, but let the medicine of silence take over. They both stared straight ahead and tried not to think about the would-be love triangle, and the repercussions that could have taken place.

After the wounds of the conversation had sufficiently healed, Geoff spoke. "So, what now?"

The question that hung in the air had so many implications that RJ dug for his one faithful escapist activity. "Let's go home. I've got a lot of work to do." He lied. The lie felt like a warm blanket. Work covered all of his many indiscretions and smoothed over the surrounding complications. The promise of a hermit life seduced him when he did not know what else to do.

The driver shook his head and smiled. "You know? You *would* work when you could be in the company of a beautiful woman. I haven't heard of you calling Adela. What happened to that whole crusade?" Geoff hooked RJ by dangling a day with Adela in front of him.

RJ took the bait, suddenly remembering the beautiful doe. His heart fluttered (of course, it was a moderately manly flutter) and he sat up straighter in his seat. "Maybe I will." The thought of seeing her again so soon made him so nervously excited that controlled RJ began fidgeting. What would they do? What would they talk about? Was there a special thing he could do to catch her eye? A myriad of questions flooded his mind as they pulled onto the final road. Even as Geoff parked the car, RJ's brain was still whirling. "Where should I take her?" He questioned his friend as he unlatched the gray seatbelt.

Geoff thought aloud. "Well there's always the inevitable conversation saver, known as dinner and a movie. You could do something very girl-weepy-movie-of-the-week and take her to your parents' graves, spending the day talking about your feelings."

"Pass. Obviously." RJ rolled his eyes.

Geoff paused as they stepped out of the car. He could hear two birds talking to each other, probably discussing the weather, and that they needed to migrate soon. The car doors slammed, doing nothing to disrupt the flow of the midday conversation going on between those two birds. Knowing RJ, Geoff offered his only quality piece of advice. "Or if you want to take off some of the pressure of being alone with her, you can always bring her around the apartment to hang out with all of us. We'll help you shine."

The idea sparkled in RJ's mind as they walked up the steps. "Yeah, I think I'll do that." He savored the thought of easing himself into dating. Just thinking about Adela made him nervous, so he gratefully took Geoff up on his offer.

Chapter Six

A grateful mindset was far from Jordan's grasp as he searched through the books in the local public library. After he had dropped Isabel off at work, he realized that he had the entire day ahead of him with nothing to do. He decided to take a trip to the library to read up on night terrors. Martha, the adorable elderly librarian, had given Jordan a list of medical journals and such to help him on his quest. Four cigarette breaks and eight books later, he had not found what he had hoped for. Only one out of the seven journals had proved to be relatively helpful, and that one book only further explained what exactly night terrors were. His mission to help his friend, he realized, was beginning to fail. After nearly four hours of searching through dusty, musty old books, Jordan surrendered to the fact that there was nothing to do but accept her gray midnight cloud, and hope that soon a night of peaceful sleep would come and erase her habit of fits. Accepting defeat with a mild frown, he returned the one semi-useful book to the library shelf, smiled at Martha and exited out into the street. A whole weekday with nothing to do, so to waste the time he decided to return to his old college habits by swinging over to Harry's Arcade. Although it had been quite some time since his last visit, he decided the venture would prove worthwhile.

Harry's Arcade was a five-minute drive to the east side of town, but Jordan took his time and made it a six-minute cruise. Walking into the arcade was an immediate sensory overload for anyone who was not as familiar with the scene as Jordan was. Bright flickering lights and loud repetitive beeps were only the tip of the iceberg. From ceiling to floor there were all sorts of random posters and trinkets. There was not an inch of white on the walls, especially since the walls had long since yellowed of their white. Even the bathroom doors were splattered with images (Bart being the mascot for the men, and Ms. Pacman escorted the women). Gigantic statues were bolted down in all sorts of random places. Superman's feet were nailed high up on the wall, with his flowing cape attached to the ceiling. King Kong (or Donkey Kong - Jordan could not decide which) was strapped in one corner, and a monstrous green Hulk foot looked like it had emerged from the wall. The whirring machines and spinning props looked as though they had been stuffed into the building. The setting was perfect - even down to the mechanical monkey riding a unicycle on a tightrope that wrapped across the entire arcade. Now Jordan was ready to relax on his day off.

Not at all distracted by the incessant noise of the games, Jordan made his way straight for the back of the store where his favorite game was located. He made one pit stop at the change machine to cash in ten dollars. Happily he shoved the forty tokens in his jacket pockets, and turned towards the Holy Grail of his youth, which was his favorite pinball machine. After placing two tarnished gold tokens into the machine, Jordan was back in play land. For as long as he could remember he had held the second highest score in the game, beating out AHT, but DrMx had always eluded him. The top three still had not changed since the last time he had visited. Although Jordan knew that it was just a game, the inner geek that lingered inside forced him to keep playing until he could beat DrMx. This, in all four years of college that he had been going to that particular arcade, had never happened. With two hours' worth of determination, he finished off all forty tokens, drawing a quaint crowd of teenage and collegiate onlookers. About eight men and one little girl watched him play with the same fervor one would use playing basketball. When the tokens ran out, he had only just matched his old score. The faithful onlookers watched with barely masked disappointment as he retyped in his name at second place.

"Man, I thought you were DrMx. You're JC?" One boy asked. Jordan nodded in reply, and the boy shook his head. "Tough break." He walked away as the small gathering dispersed. Although Jordan should have been deflated, he actually felt quite a bit lighter than he had upon entering the arcade. Even though there was one person who was better than him, he took satisfaction in knowing that he was better at that game than anyone else. Ripping off his stream of tickets from the machine, he found the little girl who had been watching him and gave them to her. He knew that neither he nor Isabel would want any of the cheap toys. Jordan played to win. He did not care about the prizes. Just knowing that his second place status was safe put a little bounce in his step as he walked past the life-sized Ninja Turtle figurine and out the double doors. The world outside of the arcade was infinitely quieter, and took a few seconds to adjust to. Glancing at his platinum wristwatch, Jordan realized that Isabel would be done working soon.

Cruising over to the pet hospital proved to be a beautiful drive. The leaves were disappearing from the tall trees, and Jordan was enjoying the chill in the breeze that slid through his slightly opened window. Breathing in the cold air made him feel alive, as if he had been hibernating that summer. The weather left him with a hankering for piping hot chocolate. This season was hot chocolate and steamy cider. Christmas was dominated by eggnog. Spring called for Jones' Root Beer with the funny labels that he liked to peel off and leave on the counter for Geoff to laugh at. Summer was the water weather, and Jordan was sick of water. As he devoured the chilled air into his lungs, he craved a mug of cocoa with a layer of marshmallows on top... and a cigarette to go with it. It was significantly colder than it had been the day before, and as Jordan pulled into the parking lot, he wondered how much longer he could wear his leather jacket before he would have to trade it in for a thick winter coat.

Instead of walking into the building, his legs decided to trot. Inside, the waiting room was much warmer, and Jordan was content as he exhaled out the last of the cold air. Isabel looked up at him as the door jingled upon his entrance. Silently, she waved, as she was on the phone with another worried pet owner. He watched her as she set up the appointment and called her boss' office to tell him that she was leaving.

Right after she hung up with her boss, the room burst with a wave of brightness as Isaac floated through the back door. "Isabel, could you help me for a minute?" Jordan immediately knew that the man must be her infamous crush, as she stammered a meek response and followed him into the back. Jordan smiled as Isaac nodded at him. He had never actually seen Isaac before, but had only heard of him when Isabel would gush about her fantasies. The way Isabel had described him, Jordan had half-expected light beams to shoot out of his fingertips. There he stood, normal. The anticlimax of finally meeting Isaac struck Jordan as quite humorous. He appeared average and unimpressive. His light blonde hair teamed with his limp wrist, and the way he balanced his weight on his right side made him appear as though Isabel had been wasting her time in pursuing him. He waited patiently for her to come back out so that he could tease her mercilessly about the pretty boy she did not have the nerve to ask out, even after years of working by his side. When she finally emerged a few minutes later, she tried to ignore the smug smile plastered across Jordan's face. Not wanting him to say anything in front of Isaac, she quickly grabbed her purse and rushed for the front entrance. "Let's go." She hurried, knowing that Jordan looked like her boyfriend instead of the friend that he was.

As soon as they reached the parking lot, Jordan let out a loud laugh. "I can't believe you! Could you want him more? What is your deal with him? He's so - " Jordan scrunched up his face with displeasure.

"Don't do the thing." She cautioned him, praying that Isaac had not noticed her friend.

"What thing?" Jordan shrugged, broadcasting his supposed innocence.

Isabel dropped her purse onto the car floor before sliding in. "The thing where you make fun of the guy until I feel stupid for liking him. Don't go there." She warned, trying not to smile at his mischievous mood.

Jordan started his car and pulled out of the parking lot. "I can't believe this is the guy that you are attracted to. What is it about him? His blonde hair? His crooked nose? The fact that he has two eyes?" Jordan joked.

"I said not to start, and look at you, starting." She set her ears on ignoring him as he rambled on. She rolled her eyes at his exaggerated body language.

"Oh, hey." Jordan interrupted the conversation about Isaac. "Did you want to take fifth home? We can swing by your coffee shop and say hi to Joe."

Isabel cleared her throat and looked out the window. "Um, Joe's gone." She had not thought about that since she had spent part of last night wandering around the street searching for him.

"Gone?" Jordan merged into the left turn lane.

"I went to go see him last night after I left you, and he was gone. I've never seen him move from that spot, so I think he might have... you know, died." She spoke the words out loud so that she could not hide from them anymore. She drew an invisible snowman on the window with her pinky finger.

Jordan did not know what to say, as he had somehow not expected this to be the homeless man's fate. Glancing at Isabel, he placed his hand on her knee. "You know, I never really understood why you had such an attachment to this random homeless guy. I mean, all you knew about him was his first name. But then when you made me bring him food the other day, I got to talk to him. I can kind of see why you'd like him. He's a great listener." Jordan offered the short-lived eulogy of the man he had met only once.

She drew a top hat on her snowman. "His name's not Joe. Well, it could be. I just made up his name. He doesn't talk." She shrugged as she stared out the window.

Jordan's eyebrows rose as he slowed down to pause at a stop sign. "What? I called him Joe! I thought that was his actual name. He must think I'm such a jerk." Jordan scolded himself.

"Oh, no. I asked him if I could call him Joe when I first met him. He doesn't care. Joe's the best." She motioned to a parking space a few yards down from the door to their building.

"You are crazy." He parked the car with ease. Jordan was an excellent parallel parker.

Neither friend said a word the whole way. Even as they walked up the stairs, they remained silent out of respect for Homeless Joe.

Isabel left Jordan to watch television on his couch, and walked into her apartment to take a shower. Everything moved rather slowly as she undressed, piece by piece. Even after she had turned on the hot water, it took a whole minute of staring at the steady stream to actually step in. The water was too hot, but Isabel did not seem to notice (or if she did notice, she did not seem to mind). With every drop that hit her, the need to cry stayed stuck in a tight lump in her throat. Swallowing it down, she tried to make peace with everything that had happened. As the steam lifted to the shampoo bubbles on her shoulders, she began the process of accepting her new life without Joe. Life without Joe was almost harder to swallow than life without her father. Somehow her new life began to feel less overwhelming as she started to make peace with the men who had left her life. Although her feet were tired after a day of working with no sleep, life slowly began to creep into her body. The need to mourn washed itself down the shower drain, and was replaced by a longing to nurture. She wanted to fill the gap in her life by giving to those few people left in her small world. As quick as a light switching on, she shut off the water and got ready for the remainder of the day in her new life. To put the seal on her new change, Isabel decided to wear her prettiest white sweater that she only wore on special occasions. It had a floppy fuzzy neck that felt like a warm hug wrapped around her. The fuzzy, snow-like bodice fit her like a glove, making her look and feel like a woman. She fully embraced her body with no dark images floating in her memory, which she had not done in a long time. She pulled on her most comfortable jeans and her extra high heels to give herself the extra edge. Forgetting that confidence does not come from clothing, she left the apartment standing a few inches taller (partly due to her confidence, the other part due to the high heels). She stuck her head into the boys' apartment; she found not just Jordan, but both roommates sitting on the kitchen stools at the counter. Both men were silently balancing silver spoons on their noses, being careful not to move. Their eyes remained crossed as they stared at their spoons.

"Uh, guys? Don't let me interrupt you. I just wanted to tell you that I'm making dinner in like, an hour or two, so don't eat." She came all the way through the door.

Very slowly Geoff raised his thumb up to her to give her the okay. "Is RJ coming home later? Where is he?" She asked two questions that required more than a simple hand gesture for clarification.

Jordan lifted his hands to show Geoff a time out. Simultaneously they took the spoons off of their noses and rubbed their eyes to made them see straight again. "Wow." Geoff's eyes settled on Isabel and came into focus. "Are you going on a date?" He had rarely ever asked her that question.

"No." She smiled.

"Are you going to church?" He set down his spoon next to Jordan's.

"No. I'm going to the grocery store. I'm making dinner tonight, so don't eat." She broadcasted a smile that showcased her new life.

"Bel, it's after seven. We already ate." Geoff informed her, rising off of his stool. "RJ's bringing Adela over later. Maybe they'll be hungry.

"What did you eat?" She huffed dramatically. "I already had my heart set on making all of us a nice dinner."

Geoff looked up at the ceiling, which was apparently where he did his best recollecting. "We had macaroni and cheese... from the box." He lifted the edge of his shirt up to show her his sucked-in belly.

"I'm actually still kind of hungry. Can I help you cook?" Jordan did his best to soothe her.

Isabel was happy again that she had a purpose. She did not have to sit around and be depressed, nor did she need soothing. She could be active and help her friends. "No." Her eyes danced as she spun on her heel and exited.

The grocery store down the street seemed a bit brighter to her that night. She thoroughly enjoyed herself as she bought her favorite foods for her dinner. She even bought a few clementines for Geoff. They were his favorite. For twenty minutes she shopped and brought home a brown grocery bag filled with food. By the time she actually got to the counter in her apartment, the overloaded bag almost gave way. Quickly unpacking, she wanted to get started before the boys came over. She locked the apartment door to stop the boys from spoiling their surprise.

An hour flew by as she cooked. Just to accentuate her good mood, she turned on one of her favorite old CDs - The Greatest Hits from the Beach Boys. The more she danced around, the more fun her cooking adventure became. She sang and shook her hips as she stuffed the mushroom caps full of herbs and sausage and breadcrumbs. Eventually the medium-sized apartment filled itself with the intoxicating scent of steak and peppers.

Her song and dance was temporarily interrupted by a knock on the door. "Are you done yet? We're really hungry." Geoff whined from the other side. "RJ and Adela are here too. Is the food ready?"

She grinned at his eagerness. "You're going to have to wait just five more minutes. I thought you weren't hungry." She teased. "I didn't make any for you." She turned off the stove and oven, transporting most of the food into nicer dishes.

"Tell me you're kidding. I'm so hungry!" He pawed at the door handle.

"Of course I'm kidding. Now go away before I make you eat on the floor." She banged the oil off of her wooden spoon.

While the steaks were sizzling, Isabel set the table with actual dishes - not paper plates. She even lit a tall ivory candle and traded The Beach Boys for Bach. After she put the rest of the food onto the table, the dinner was ready to be eaten. Before she called everyone in to eat, she took a quiet moment to reflect and look at the table laden with food. She had taken precious effort to prepare it all, and staring at the food in front of her made her actually want to consume it. The wealth of food on the table brought a certain level of contentment to her heart. Knowing that she had cooked all of it by herself made her feel strong, like nothing was too big for her. This moment of calm lasted more than a minute in her mind. It was the mark of her new start, and she new that now she was ready for the change.

Taking a deep breath, she unlocked the door to call them over. She took one more look back at the table and sighed. Taking three steps out of the apartment, she knocked on her friends' door. "Come on over." She called.

No sooner had the words escaped her mouth, than the door flung open with Geoff standing behind it. "Is it ready?" He trotted over next to her.

"Yeah." She nodded.

The second he stepped into the apartment, his mouth watered. "Oh man, I'm starving." With his eyes as big as golf balls, he took in the whole scene. There were candles, music, actual dishes, and no sign of any pasta meals that may have come from a box. "Why don't you do this all the time? This is nice!" He rubbed her back warmly.

Jordan, RJ and Adela trailed into the elegantly decorated dinner with mouths wide open. Adela tugged on Isabel's sleeve. "I can leave if you want. I don't want to put you out." She whispered shyly.

Isabel squeezed her hand and rubbed her arm. "No sweetie, the guys told me that you two would be here. I set you a place next to RJ. I hope we aren't ruining your date." The sudden concern set upon her.

The boys were in the midst of quietly teasing RJ as the girls whispered to each other. "Oh, not at all. I'm actually sort of nervous, so this is great. Thanks so much." She looked at Isabel and smiled the grateful smile of a girl who needed a new sister.

"Come on, women. Let's eat!" Jordan motioned for them to sit down. As he waved his hand to bring them to the table, he accidentally dipped his shirtsleeve in the gravy dish as he brought his elbow back down. "Aw, man!" He looked around to see if anyone had witnessed his miniature blunder. Sure enough, everyone at the table was staring at his gravy-soaked sleeve. Instead of caring, he shrugged his shoulders. "Oh well, at least Geoff washed this shirt. I'd be more upset if I had washed it myself and then stained it." He explained, taking off the now dirty shirt.

Isabel trotted into RJ's room to grab another shirt for Jordan to wear. "Don't kid yourself, I did your laundry." She ruffled Geoff's hair as she sat down. "Are we ready to eat?"

The chatter quieted down, but the lull was immediately ruptured by a knock on the door. Isabel stood up to answer the door, and found none other than her all too familiar ex-boyfriend standing before her. Instead of responding in her usual hostile manner, she swallowed her sarcastic welcome that she had all set in place to fire at him. "Hi, Donny. Come on in." Donny was just as shocked as most of the people sitting at the table were. "It's nice to see you." She commented, nearly bowling her brother out of his chair with her sudden change. "Are you hungry?"

Donny looked around the room for any signs of hidden video cameras or anvils that could fall on him from the sky. "Sure. Thanks, Isabel." He looked at her with one more ounce of the self-esteem he had lost when she cut him out of her life. "What's going on, guys?" He entered the candlelit room, sure that he must have broken into some alternate reality by mistake.

Isabel pulled her own chair out for him to sit in. "Have a seat." She insisted, shocking all of the men in the room. Bewildered, Donny took her place at the table. He could not help but wonder if something truly horrible was about to happen to compensate for the goodness coming from the woman who usually despised him. She set another place at the table and smiled at all four of the shocked men staring at her. Not willing to let this dinner be awkward, Isabel began chatting about work as she passed the food around. Soon, everyone temporarily forgot how strange it all was as they stuffed their mouths with the delicious food. After they had all finished, Adela and RJ volunteered to do the dishes. The boys gaped at the notion that RJ would clean anything, but kept this comment between them as they moved into the living room.

Geoff's eyes lit up. "Oh, I have the best dessert!" He jogged into his own apartment, and came back with the big bag of suckers.

RJ rolled his eyes. "You can't be serious." He moaned at Geoff.

Geoff ignored his friend as he explained the purpose of this new game. "But you have to keep track." He insisted, pulling out a pad of paper and a few pens from the appropriately titled "junk drawer".

Isabel turned on a movie as she allowed herself the luxury of curling up comfortably in Jordan's lap. All six friends sat around the coffee table in the living room with their pens and paper, divvying up the suckers.

"Here you go, Bel." Geoff tore off the last piece of paper from the pad he was using and handed it up to her. "What color do you want?" He pointed to the bag on the coffee table.

Isabel cracked an elated smile at her strange friends and reached for an orange sucker. When she leaned back, she snuggled her head into the crook of Jordan's neck and tickled it with a soft kiss as she unwrapped her sucker. "Orange?" Jordan blushed and tried to hide the chill that spiked through him by taking her sucker with a look of disgust. "Nobody likes orange. Orange is the color you get stuck with after everyone else gets what they want. Isabel, there's plenty of colors left. Don't pick the gross one." He rested his chin on her head, relieved that she was still comfortable in his arms. He was afraid that with all of her changing, that she might not fit there anymore. Smelling the top of her head caused his eyes to close. She smelled like sexy woman and beef, which caused him to groan aloud with pleasure. He allowed himself to notice how suggestively attractive she looked on his lap.

Taking her sucker back from his grasp, she wrinkled her nose at his comment. "I love orange."

She took her first lick and instantly recalled how fun it was to be a child. With each lick that she took, she was brought further and further back to that protected place of innocence where all the pieces in her life made sense to each other. She watched her friends lick their suckers, all sitting together and joking around like there had never been a rough spot they had ever been forced to cross. Taking in her twenty-second lick, Isabel wrapped up her sucker and tossed it onto the coffee table. Jordan did the same so that he could enclose both of his strong arms around the woman he secretly loved. Kissing his unshaven cheek, Isabel cuddled in closer to his strong body.

Experiencing peace that she had not ever remembered feeling before, she closed her heavy eyes and allowed herself to rest.

Printed in the United States
209448BV00002B/19/P

9 780615 260648